Praise for

SUPERSURVIVORS

APR 15

"Turns out surviving the most dangerous situations has some good lessons we can use to learn how to be resilient in everyday life."

— *Time Magazine* online

"Fascinating . . . ultimately, we discover our ability to deal with unforeseen challenges and realize the remarkable potential of the human spirit."

— *Psychology Today*

"If you read Feldman and Kravetz, you will come away inspired and more attuned to the factors that influence resilience—including religious faith, the ability to forgive, and awareness of mortality."

— *Harvard Business Review*

"*Supersurvivors* is a brilliant rethinking of the consequences of trauma. This book will change the meaning we give to survival, both for individuals and for our culture as a whole."

— Ethan Watters, author of *Crazy Like Us:*
The Globalization of the American Psyche

"Just surviving suffering is a form of success. But these people have done more than survive, and their stories are worth your time. One day you may need what they have."

— Linda Ellerbee, Peabody and Emmy Award winner,
New York Times bestselling author

"A charming and thoughtful mix of scientific thought and anecdotal evidence."

— *Mindful* magazine

"In *Supersurvivors*, Feldman and Kravetz create an inspiring narrative that elegantly integrates compelling personal stories, evidence-based conclusions, myth busting, and their keen insights to help solve a core problem of human nature: how some of us bounce back from disaster and adversity to thrive while creating even more vibrant lives. Learn those secrets here. Read on."

— Philip Zimbardo, PhD, *New York Times*
bestselling author of *The Lucifer Effect*

"This is a blockbuster that every leader, parent, doctor, teacher, student, coach, and caregiver needs to read. I can't remember the last time I was so fascinated and moved by a book—let alone one grounded in science."

— Adam Grant, professor at the Wharton School of Business,
New York Times bestselling author of *Give and Take*

"*Supersurvivors* might well be a how-to manual on taking adversity and turning it into an advantage. As I read it, I kept thinking: I wish I'd had this book ten years ago!"

— Aron Ralston, survivor, speaker, author,
subject of the film *127 Hours*

"This is the rare work that is both profound and accessible. The joint effort of a scholar and journalist presents the most complex of ideas in the most human of ways on one of humanity's most urgent problems. I read this work with tears and laughter, with anguish and with hope."

— Michael Berenbaum, project director of the United States
Holocaust Memorial Museum (1988–1993)

"It's rare to find a book that appeals so well to both the head and the heart. Marrying eye-opening stories with thought-provoking science, Feldman and Kravetz open a powerful window into a world of forgiveness and hope."

— Frederic Luskin, PhD, author of *Forgive for Good*,
director of the Stanford Forgiveness Project

SUPERSURVIVORS

ALSO BY DAVID B. FELDMAN

*The End-of-Life Handbook: A Compassionate Guide to
Connecting with and Caring for a Dying Loved One*

*Public Speaking for Psychologists: A Lighthearted Guide to
Research Presentation, Job Talks, and Other Opportunities
to Embarrass Yourself*

SUPERSURVIVORS

The Surprising Link between

Suffering and Success

David B. Feldman, PhD, *and* Lee Daniel Kravetz

HARPER WAVE

An Imprint of HarperCollins*Publishers*

HarperCollins books may be purchased for educational, business, or sales promotional use. For information, please e-mail the Special Markets Department at SPsales@harpercollins.com.

A hardcover edition of this book was published in 2014 by HarperWave, an imprint of HarperCollins Publishers.

FIRST HARPERWAVE PAPERBACK EDITION PUBLISHED 2015

Designed by Jaime Putorti

Library of Congress Cataloging-in-Publication Data has been applied for.

ISBN: 978-0-06-226786-3 (pbk.)

15 16 17 18 19   OV/RRD   10 9 8 7 6 5 4 3 2 1

For my parents, who taught me how to hope.

—DAVID B. FELDMAN

For Mimi. You were right.

—LEE DANIEL KRAVETZ

Contents

1

To Survive or to Supersurvive

To destroy is always the first step in any creation.
—E. E. CUMMINGS, SUPERSURVIVOR

On the spectrum of trauma survivorship, everyone falls somewhere between hiding under a rock and becoming a rock star.

Asha Mevlana lay on a table in a small examination room at Saint Vincent Catholic Medical Center in the West Village, New York City, when this first crossed her mind. She was twenty-four years old, dark-haired, and beautiful. The technology industry in 2002 was making young people all over the city rich. She had a great job at a start-up, an apartment in SoHo, and a pearl-shaped problem within her left breast.

Asha had already guessed that it was cancer; the lab technician's grim look was merely confirmation. The defining moment of her ordeal, however, wasn't the diagnosis. It wasn't the biopsy at Sloan Kettering. It also wasn't the undeniable sensation that her life was spinning out of control as she underwent eight months of chemotherapy. It wasn't her baldness or her candle-wax pallor, either.

For Asha, the defining moment came after the doctors announced that she was cancer-free and sent her back out into the world. She noticed that something within her had changed. While she'd been facing her mortality, everyone else had gone on blithely living their lives. Her coworkers talked about the crummy New York weather, the long lines at Starbucks, and the finalists on *American Idol*. The blissfully mundane events of their lives seemed to diminish the most significant and defining experience of hers. Everyone seemed to place value in such inconsequential things, and she found herself yearning for a time when she did as well.

Life as Asha once knew it simply didn't make sense anymore; it seemed empty. So, she promptly dropped out of it. "I'm not a religious person, but I prayed: 'Just give me a second chance and I'm going to change my life. I'm going to do what I'm passionate about,'" she says.

———

Asha is not alone.

According to the American Cancer Society, roughly thirteen million people around the world are diagnosed with cancer each year, a number that is projected to double in the next two decades. The journal *Neuroimaging Clinics of North America* provides a similarly grim outlook, with a startling ten million people worldwide affected every year by traumatic brain injuries. The harsh reality of widespread trauma becomes even more apparent once we combine these numbers with the World Health Organization's calculation that fifty million people a year survive car wrecks; the United Nations' finding that one out of every three women will be beaten, raped, or otherwise abused during her lifetime; and the realization that these statistics cover only a small portion of the catastrophes that befall people every day.

It is no coincidence that the seeds of this book took root during a particular point in history, one that could be fairly characterized as traumatic for a lot of people. America's housing bubble ruptured, global markets plummeted, millions of people lost jobs and homes, the Tohoku earthquake shifted the earth on its axis by more than six inches, and as acts of terrorism spiked, people found themselves grasping for a sense of safety. These days, such events are practically the backdrop of daily life.

Harvard Medical School professor of psychiatry Judith Herman calls trauma "the affliction of the powerless." The problem is we're all powerless against the vicissitudes of fate. "At the moment of trauma, the victim is rendered helpless by an overwhelming force. When the force is that of nature, we speak of disasters. When the force is that of other human beings, we speak of atrocities," she writes in her book *Trauma and Recovery*. "Traumatic events are extraordinary, not because they occur rarely, but rather because they overwhelm the ordinary human adaptations to life." Depending on the particular type of trauma, about a quarter of survivors will fall into posttraumatic stress disorder, a painful and often debilitating condition. Others will experience significant depression or anxiety.

In the midst of all this adversity, it's tempting to become pessimistic and fall into a kind of fatalistic hopelessness. It's easy to overlook the amazing potential for resilience in us as human beings. Amazingly, even in midst of trauma, people continue to smile, to love, to celebrate, to create, and to renew. In making this observation, we absolutely do not mean to belittle the impact of traumatic times or the suffering many have endured and continue to endure. Suffering is real, but resilience is also real. It is an incredible and encouraging fact about human nature that, contrary to popular belief, after a period of emotional turmoil, most trauma survivors eventually recover and return to their lives. They bounce back.

And in some cases, they do much more. They bounce *forward*, and in truly remarkable ways. "A significant minority, as a result of the trauma, feel called upon to engage in a wider world," Herman writes. They refocus their energies on a new calling, on a new mission, on a new path, on helping others who have been victimized, on education, on legal reforms, or any number of other big goals. They move beyond mere resilience. They transform the meaning of their personal tragedies by making them the bases for change.

We call these people supersurvivors.

——

In the aftermath of her cancer diagnosis, Asha paid for improvisational violin lessons. Her teacher took a unique approach with her. "She asked me to play how I felt the day I walked into the hospital to get treatments," she explains. "She didn't want me to use any words, just my instrument. It was the first time I felt close to my instrument and was actually able to improvise from my heart. Looking back, I was actually meditating on my instrument. I played the anxiety I felt when they injected the needle into my arm that contained the chemo. I played about trying to be strong for everyone else, even though I was terrified. I learned how to express myself through my instrument."

Before surviving her trauma, Asha had no illusions about making a career out of music. "You mean like playing for bar tips? No, it never crossed my mind. I was just way too practical," she remembers. But that pragmatism didn't survive the chemotherapy. After working hard for many months, she began playing electric violin for a few amateur rock bands. This was a new and invigorating experience for her; she hadn't hung out with people like this before. All her friends were either investment bankers or corporate suits. Something about this new life clicked. Perhaps it was the unscripted nature that, much like the music itself, was creative and freeing. A couple of months later, when a friend invited her to visit Los Angeles for a weekend, she met a number of local musicians who convinced her she could get paying gigs in California.

Before her cancer Asha believed, like many, that mature adults should settle into a routine life and count their blessings. "I wouldn't have ever told anyone I really wanted to be a rock violinist," she says. "Nobody even knew what that was, but it was always in the back of my head. I'd never taken any risks before. Everything I'd ever done had been very calculated. I stuck to things I knew I'd be successful at."

It would be an enormous risk. Asha's entire universe was on the East Coast. She had no job prospects in Los Angeles, no income, no place to live, and a million reasons to go back to her old life. Plus, although proficient in violin, she was safely an amateur.

Then again, she was twenty-eight years old, one of the youngest survivors of breast cancer she knew, spiritually damaged, and more than a little lost. From this perspective, she had nothing to lose.

So, in 2007 she moved to L.A., tugged by a desire not uncommon to those with the predilection for chasing something bright and shiny and unpredictable. Strolling along the Sunset Strip, a slipstream of bright neon signs fastened to beer-soaked bars and windowless strip clubs, she felt her corporate cubicle fade into pale memory.

In the origin stories of superheroes, something profound, unexpected, and often frightening transforms ordinary lives. A massive discharge of radiation turns a mild-mannered scientist into a hulking green avenger; the murder of another's parents leads him to don a black mask and dedicate his life to rescuing innocent victims of a maniacal joker. What if these scenarios are closer to reality than we think?

According to nearly two decades of research emerging from institutions as far-flung as the University of North Carolina, Charlotte, and the University of Warwick, England, the majority of trauma survivors reports some degree of positive change. These individuals may emerge from otherwise awful experiences primed with something like X-ray vision, which allows them to notice value and opportunity where they might never have seen them before. They may develop inner strength from having lived through an experience beyond their worst imaginings. These psychological gains are known as posttraumatic growth.

But even after experiencing such inner growth, most trauma survivors find their outer lives returning to normal. According to research, the majority of posttraumatic growth is internal and private. It's what psychologists refer to as perceived growth. Survivors report that they've changed for the better, and they may feel the benefits of that change, but outwardly their lives don't look much different from before the trauma. Perceived growth isn't fake, however. Though the research is mixed, some studies show links between greater perceived growth and lower emotional distress as well as better physical health.

But sometimes people move far beyond both the life-altering negative effects of trauma and the usual outcomes of perceived posttraumatic growth. These people don't just grow; they revolutionize their lives. They transform and transcend their suffering even while enduring it. These supersurvivors radically deviate from their previous life paths, often transforming the worst thing that's happened to them into the best.

—————

Asha has a kick-ass Viper electric violin. It's purple, and the hourglass-shaped belly is cleaved. Instead of the classic configuration of four strings, Asha's fingerboard is laced with seven. Rachmaninoff would have been puzzled but awed.

One afternoon Asha picked up her violin from a repair shop in downtown Los Angeles. The guy who had made her instrument said he knew Dee Snider, the lead singer of Twisted Sister, who just happened to be trying out electric violinists to join his new tour. Although she thought her chances were slim, Asha auditioned. Two months later, she celebrated her thirtieth birthday on a tour bus with one of the top metal vocalists of all time.

One opportunity led to the next. With startling swiftness, Asha was hired to play alongside Alanis Morissette, and after that, on a U.S. tour with Gnarls Barkley, opening for the Red Hot Chili Peppers in front of thirty thousand people a night. That same year, she performed at the Grammys. Jay Z and Mary J. Blige both tapped her to play. Her reputation on the rise, in 2009 she played regularly for the *American Idol* band and *The Tonight Show*.

Working under the nurturing wings of music godparents Linda Perry, Holly Knight, and Mike Chapman, she was now on the brink of mainstream success with her own band, Porcelain, which was newly signed to Universal Music, the same powerhouse label that represented Rihanna and the Black Eyed Peas.

Asha had been in Los Angeles fifteen months. If someone had told her in New York that someday she'd be playing in front of millions of people and signed to a major recording label, she'd have laughed in disbelief. Yet she'd arrived at this place with unusual calm, as though somewhere in the back of her mind she always knew she'd wind up here. It just took surviving a cataclysmic event for her to reassemble the pieces of her life into something that exceeded her wildest dreams.

———

Asha is one of many people we'll meet who have dramatically altered their lives after suffering trauma, often discovering hidden parts of themselves or contributing to the world in ways they never thought possible. But these people are not superheroes—at least, no more than any other trauma survivor. In truth, they aren't even superhuman. Their stories betray their utter humanness—their stumbling and their grasping as they wrestle with the fundamental questions we all face: Who am I? What do I believe in? And most important, how should I live my life? There is a lot we can learn from their often haphazard but beautiful answers to these questions.

To be clear, this is not a book extolling the bright side of tragedy, the silver lining of any cloud, or the so-called "power of positive thinking." No trauma is good. Every trauma involves suffering. There is nothing inherently positive or indispensable about atrocities, violence, disasters, or illness.

Given that such events are sometimes unavoidable, it is important to understand the incredible resilience possible for ordinary human beings—an ability to peer into the face of tragedy and somehow emerge fundamentally changed and able to impact the world in previously unimagined ways. Drawing from research in the fields of psychology, psychiatry, sociology, anthropology, and even business, in this book we explore why and how people transform suffering into personal triumph. Each chapter focuses on a particular principle of change identified by social scientists, including hope, personal control, social support, forgiveness, and spirituality.

But these principles don't always work the way you'd think. We explore how hope has little to do with positive thinking, and how, despite conventional wisdom, the disorientation and groundlessness experienced by many people after trauma can ultimately be advantageous. We discover why psychologists think that certain delusions can be healthy, why forgiveness is good for one's physiology as well as for the soul, and why reflecting on death can lead to a better life. From the inspiring stories presented in this book, we might believe that supersurvivors have it good—that their trauma was somehow a stroke of luck. We ask supersurvivors what they think about this supposed good fortune and come to some eye-opening conclusions. Finally, we ask what implications their stories have for the rest of us, regardless of whether we've survived a serious trauma or are merely confronting the setbacks and difficulties of everyday life.

The personal struggles and triumphs of survivors inspire fascination. We would be deceiving ourselves if we didn't acknowledge that some of this fascination is due to the normal voyeuristic tendencies present in all of us. Beyond these base impulses, however, lie more venerable motivations. As all of us grapple with the adversities of our chaotic times, we are increasingly aware of human suffering and the fragility of our own prosperity. We may wonder, "What would I do if a crisis were to strike close to home?" Supersurvivors provide unexpected answers to this question—their stories offer hope that trauma can lead to growth and transcendence, and that fear of tragedy doesn't have to cause us to shrink from a full and adventurous life. Their examples can uplift us, nourish our tender emotions, and inspire us to grow, no matter who we are or what we've been through.

Asha's cancer experience was a transformative and meaningful turning point. It afforded her the freedom and motivation to move beyond her previous life and build a new reality for herself. Instead of hampering her, trauma freed her. But stories like Asha's aren't typical. While trauma leaves many people suffering, lost, and searching to reclaim their lives, Asha's experience seems to have provided her with direction.

In this book, we discover why.

2

The Paradox of Positive Thinking

What we call the beginning is often the end.
And to make an end is to make a beginning.
The end is where we start from.
—T. S. ELIOT

On a blustery winter morning, Alan Lock stepped out onto the balcony of his tiny hotel room set below the high cliffs of La Gomera, one of Spain's lush Canary Islands. For days the rain had come down in hard sheets. Today, just beyond the hotel, the ocean was calm, and the air was warm against his skin. Alan rubbed his eyes and squinted sharply against the muted sunlight.

In his late twenties, Alan had a narrow face punctuated with a re-served grin. His hair was the color of wet sand. Around noon that day, his buddy Matt Boreham, a big guy with dark hair and an adventurous streak, examined the weather conditions and announced it was time to go. Alan pulled a pair of shorts over a reedy frame that scarcely reflected his decade's worth of military training and donned a T-shirt, sun visor, and sunglasses.

Off the marina's long pier, the ocean was simmering and grow-ing choppy. The stiffening wind was pushing *Gemini*'s twenty-four-foot white hull up against the dock. The vessel was built to sustain the ocean's full blunt force, but its large plywood hull and blocky bulkhead made maneuvering the boat tricky. On board, Alan set his bags down in the cramped cargo compartment and took first position in the rowboat's cockpit, a command center as narrow as a bathtub. As Matt released the nylon tether and tied off the cleat, Alan stiffened his back and tugged with both arms, raking two long oars across the surface of the water. It was the first stride in what would be a three-thousand-mile journey across the Atlantic Ocean.

The goal was to leave La Gomera and row to Barbados. They had enough food for a hundred days. By Alan's calculations, if the ocean cooperated, they'd be there in fewer than seventy—a good thing, because they were racing hurricane season. Many had attempted, unsuccessfully, to row this route, including Alan's navigator, Matt. More people had traveled to outer space than paddled across the Atlantic. It was a dangerous course to take with no motor, no sail, just five-by-seven feet of maneuvering space, a compass, a GPS, and gas-powered cooking supplies, and one significant disadvantage that no one in recorded history had dealt with during such a journey: Alan Lock was attempting to become the first registered blind person ever to row one of the world's oceans.

If you listened to Alan's fans, you'd think he did it all with the power of positive thinking. It's the kind of story often burnished with terms such as *bravery* and *inspiration*. *The New York Times* called him "remarkable." *The Faster Times* and the BBC alluded to his extraordinary optimism. In most versions of the story, Alan's loss of vision in 2003 served only to strengthen his resolve and multiply his natural athletic gifts. Alan's story seems like a perfect example of what positive thinking in the face of tragedy can help a person achieve.

But Alan has a secret. Spend a few minutes with him and you'll hear him say things like "I always expect the worst" and "I knew I was doomed." No matter how many people attest to Alan's remarkable attitude in the face of great adversity, he'll tell you he's a pessimist. "I'm just not a silver-lining kind of person," he insists.

―――――

Conventional wisdom says that positive thinking after a tragedy leads to better outcomes. When the bottom drops out, having a rosy attitude is better than thinking the worst, right? Yet for more than half a century psychologists have debated this facile version of "the power of positive thinking."

Those arguing for this perspective assert that positive thinking is nothing less than an antidote to threatening illness and the secret to achieving success in life. Thank mid-twentieth-century Protestant preacher Norman Vincent Peale for this view. His book *The Power of Positive Thinking* offered a doctrine gilded by an appealing promise: positive thinking can bring about positive realities. This assertion has been a jumping-off point for scores of self-help books extolling positive thinking as the secret to fortune. Some have even asserted that it is the key to cheating death. Self-help books and inspirational leaders have made many claims, including "Thoughts equal creation: If these thoughts are attached to powerful emotions (good or bad), that speeds the creation"; "You attract your dominant thoughts. Those who speak most of illness have illness, those who speak most of prosperity have it"; and "Positive attitude can even overcome serious diseases like diabetes, arthritis, and heart conditions."

In 2006, David Schweingruber of Iowa State University's Department of Sociology provided some evidence in support of this theory by following employees of the Enterprise Company, a pseudonym for one of the oldest door-to-door sales outfits in the United States. The Enterprise Company was especially perfect for this task for one reason: for years it made use of something the company called "emotional training." Among other practices, the company encouraged its employees to read self-help books, repeat scripted positive phrases, and commit their goals to paper.

Guess what happened? Enterprise employees sold more than thirty million dollars' worth of products to nearly three hundred

thousand customers over the course of a summer—an unbeliev-
ably impressive total. The study suggested that a positive attitude
works.

But could success really be that simple? These salespeople were
a special group of highly motivated achievers who knew what they
were getting into when they joined the Enterprise Company. They
were naturally drawn to a firm steeped in positive thinking and were
prodded by the desire to make money. Perhaps it wasn't the strategies
they employed that led these salespeople to success; perhaps it was
just *who they were*. If positive thinking is really such an easy recipe
for success, why do so many businesses fail?

———

When he joined the Royal Navy, Alan Lock told his recruitment
officer, "My worst fear in life is being stuck behind a desk." Alan knew
as a kid he was going to be a career military man. Starting with the
final two years of his secondary education, the Royal Air Force spon-
sored him to be a navigation officer.

Night watch on the destroyer HMS *York* failed to employ his extensive training in navigation, but as a junior officer he took these
assignments seriously. His shifts were long, and by the end, his body
felt heavy. On one such night, he could barely read the print on his
navigation charts. He wondered if it was fatigue that made the text
blur across the page. Oddly, come morning, he still couldn't read the
charts, and now his eyes ached. As the weeks passed, phantom shad-
ows spirited behind objects. Gaps blinked in and out of his field of
vision. He was swimming in panic.

Alan went in for eye testing, and the results that came back were
startling. He had been born with a genetic abnormality, a chromo-
somal mutation that affects a part of the eye related to fine detail,
the macula. Over time, macular degeneration gradually drowns the
life of cells in the tissue of the retina, the part of the eye that detects

luminosity and color. People in their sixties and seventies ordinarily get the disease. Alan was twenty-three.

When he asked his physician about treatment, he received yet another blow. There was none. Moments passed in silence. He would never fully see again, never drive again, never read again.

Alan tried to keep his mind on the positive. He pored through the medical research, and nowhere did it say he was doomed to go *completely* blind. The rate of degeneration had slowed. His vision loss might stabilize. As far as his future with the Royal Navy was concerned, there might be positions that didn't require perfect vision. He'd request a transfer. Yes, he tried to tell himself, everything would be fine.

Two months after his diagnosis, however, Alan followed the sound of a clerical officer's footsteps into a small room bathed in thin wintery light. At a tiny desk, he was handed a hefty stack of pages. The type was too small to read, just a sea of gray smudge. But he didn't need to make out any words of this letter of liability to know what it said. He was losing his military career.

This wasn't just a rejection of his skills or a repudiation of his dreams and hard work. "The worst part is that I didn't have a heroic story to tell," he says. "It's such an ignoramus end!" Not that he'd anticipated a brutal, bloody finale, but at that moment, this felt worse.

People tried to encourage him. So, he tried hard to remain positive, to project a brave and hopeful image. He searched hard for reasons to be optimistic. Despite his best efforts, however, he could not find a silver lining. What he felt wasn't optimism. It was anger and immense frustration, both focused on the inevitable imperfection—smaller than a bullet—that had taken him out of the game before the game had even gotten started. "I wouldn't be human if I didn't feel a sense of despair," he says. "Try to compete on a level playing field, and anyway you cut it, being blind isn't an advantage. I thought maybe I'd get vision back and my old job, but life just kind of kept letting me down. I felt helpless."

The world was slipping into a blurry pageant. Alan had now lost the majority of his useful vision. The periphery of his visual field remained fine—such is the nature of the disease—while his center vision was like looking through milky frosted glass. As his eyesight declined, so did his independence.

This was where Alan found himself when positive thinking most failed him. "No matter what people say, there were no positives in losing my sight," he says. "You might stretch it and say you appreciate your hearing; you might say, 'Keep your head up, and think about what all these other blind people do to get by.' But I'd have given anything to change this."

But Alan is obviously much more than simply a pessimist, especially given what he would accomplish. He may not believe in the simplistic kind of positive thinking so often advocated in popular culture, but he isn't exactly promoting negative thinking, either. "Thinking realistically," he says, "it was the only way to move forward."

———

Alan's claim mirrors the research. Telling yourself, "Everything will be fine" or "It will all be okay" if it probably won't may undermine your ability to take action to make your situation better. For decades, psychologists and public health researchers have been interested in what makes people take steps to head off disasters. Why, for instance, do some people go in for colonoscopies or mammograms while others don't? After all, these relatively simple procedures could help prevent horrible tragedies. Perhaps the most prominent perspective on this issue is called the health belief model. According to the health belief model, a number of factors predict whether someone will take a risk, but two of the most important are perceived susceptibility and perceived severity. In short, if we believe that a particular action will put us at risk of harm, and that the harm is severe enough, we probably won't take that action. Likewise, if we think a particular action is likely to protect us from harm, we'll probably take that action. These two factors have found support in dozens of studies. The health belief model has been shown to predict health-promoting behaviors such as seeking out cancer screening, engaging in safer sex, eating a heart-healthy diet, and getting the flu vaccination; it has even been shown to predict lower levels of criminal behavior.

Not surprisingly, one of the major criticisms of this theory is that it's common sense—and it is.

But what does this mean for positive thinking? In short, people who pay attention to the positives at the expense of noticing the potential for negatives, who believe that everything is (or will be) fine despite their being at real risk, may not take appropriate action to protect themselves. Their lack of belief in their own susceptibility may be dangerous.

Back in 2008 an intriguing war of philosophies brought this issue some prominence. It started with Dutch marathon swimmer Maarten van der Weijden. By age nineteen, Maarten was already a regional swimming champion. Nonetheless, when recalling that time in his life, he is filled with intense ambivalence.

"When young people are good at sports, others encourage them to pursue it. The child is not making that choice. Others get the ball rolling for the child, and the easiest thing for that child to do is just keep doing it. And if you're really good, they tell you, you can win the Olympics someday," he explains from his home in Rotterdam. And Maarten believed them. "But now I see I hadn't been a realistic person. The odds of me competing and winning in something like the Olympics someday was just pie-in-the-sky thinking and based entirely on false hope." The fact is, as young Maarten looked around, he noticed that other athletes were naturally more gifted than he. The overly positive statements of his family and friends seemed to ignore this obvious fact, leading Maarten to feel alienated from his biggest supporters.

His early swimming career would be abruptly halted, however, by acute lymphoblastic leukemia, a potentially fatal illness.

In sports, Maarten didn't meet a lot of realistic people, and he didn't meet a lot of realistic people in the hospital, either. As in swimming, in the cancer ward many believed that positive thinking would give one patient an edge over another, but Maarten felt they were all too ready to provide false hope. Although he recognized that his odds of surviving were about 30 percent, friends would tell him not to think about his low chances and to keep his mind only on the positive. "There was a big gap between my idea of hope and their ideas of hope," Maarten notes. "For me, hope was chemotherapy. It was science. When you think of it this way, it's really weird to say positive thinking helps you."

"When I was young, my father tried to teach me everything was possible if I worked hard and thought about it right," he continues. "For a long time I believed him. But when I got sick, it was the first time in my life I didn't."

Maarten simply couldn't tell himself that everything would be okay. He felt strongly that he must admit to himself the reality of what was happening. Only then could he begin taking steps to deal with it.

Although Maarten's family and friends were deeply concerned by his peculiarly un-positive attitude, it hardly destroyed him. Based on his realistic, if not very rosy, understanding of the situation, he began to set small goals for himself, goals to get through the week alive, to get through the day with minimal pain, to survive the next round of chemotherapy, to make it through the stem cell transplant that ultimately saved his life. Three years later and cancer-free, he slipped back into a swimming pool.

This time, however, he decided to run his swimming career using the same brand of realistic yet forward-looking thinking that had gotten him through his leukemia. "I knew the odds of success were very small," he says. "I knew that I was not the fastest swimmer. I would have to train extra hard to get back to the level I was at before my illness, and even harder just to overcome my own natural shortfalls. Instead of gunning for an international championship, as I had as a youth, I set out simply to swim my best in small competitions."

Over the next five years, he qualified for the World Open Water Swimming Championships in Barcelona, winning three Dutch titles in the 800-meter and 1500-meter freestyle competitions. Following World Cup wins in Ismaila, Pakistan; Al Fujairah and Dubai, United Arab Emirates; and Argentina, and a World Championship title in Seville, he qualified to compete in the 2008 Olympics in Beijing. Knowing that he wasn't the quickest or strongest athlete present, he swam at the back of the pack, avoiding the slipstream, and at the last moment pulled ahead, clinching the gold.

To outside observers, Maarten's comeback seemed amazing. Among his biggest supporters was none other than the prime minister of the Netherlands, Jan Pieter Balkenende. "He called me an inspiration," Maarten says. But Maarten believed he was not a hero; he'd simply survived a trauma. And as for getting cancer, in his mind it had nothing to do with his winning the gold. However, the media continued to compare Maarten to another famous cancer survivor.

"Don't call me Lance Armstrong!" Maarten insists.

Maarten had nothing personal against Armstrong, who was at the peak of his fame and respect at the time. What he took offense to was a string of statements the world-renowned cyclist and cancer survivor had made over the years about positive attitude, survival, and victory. "Without cancer, I never would have won a single Tour de France," Armstrong wrote. In an interview on *CBS Sunday Morning*, the cyclist added, "You can't deny the fact that a person with a positive and optimistic attitude does a lot better."

In a widely circulated 2008 interview with London's *The Daily Telegraph*, Maarten very publically denied this. "Armstrong says that positive thinking and doing a lot of sports can save you. I don't agree."

He then added, "I even think it's dangerous."

———

Maarten felt the public's backlash immediately.

Detractors relied on empirical evidence that seemed to support the idea that positive thinking was a key to successfully surviving serious illness. Studies show links between positive psychological well-being and reduced death by heart attack as well as reduced death rates in patients with various life-threatening illnesses.

People often take news like this to mean that positive thinking has been explicitly proven to be good for your health. If it sounds too good to be true, it might be. The truth, much like Alan's and Maarten's stories imply, appears to be more complicated.

University of Pennsylvania psychologist James Coyne wondered how firm such conclusions were, particularly as they related to patients with cancer. In the journal *Psychosomatic Medicine*, Coyne writes, "Are we prepared to accept that the effects of any one or more psychosocial 'protective factors' will overwhelm risks of poor outcome attributable to disease severity variables?" So, he and his team undertook a careful examination of the previous research. This wasn't a cursory look at the results, but rather a critical evaluation of the methodology that produced those results. They wanted to know whether these astounding findings were based on sound research techniques.

It turns out that Coyne arrived at conclusions very similar to Maarten's. In articles published in *Annals of Behavioral Medicine* and *Psychological Bulletin*, Coyne and his team reported finding major flaws in much of the research. Technically speaking, many of the studies made use of small samples, lacked clearly specified hypotheses, or used inappropriate methods to analyze the data and interpret the results. Put in plain English, the conclusion that positive thinking affects survival, Coyne suggested, was based on biased or at least flawed research.

To be fair, almost all studies have flaws. That doesn't mean anybody has done anything wrong. But if a great deal of the research has major methodological flaws, as Coyne proposes, it's possible that positive thinking isn't as powerful as a lot of people think. That's not to say that positive thinking is never helpful under any circumstances. Everyone knows that you can find exceptions to any rule if you look in the right places. But what's the rule? What works for most people?

Coyne alluded to one more thing in his *Annals of Behavioral Medicine* article: there may be an inherent danger in elevating positive thinking to too powerful a position, a danger that Maarten spent quite some time considering while battling his cancer. "I think we believe a cancer patient has a lot of influence himself because we want to believe that," Maarten said in his TEDx speech in 2010. "It's a nice thought for the patient, for people who love that patient, and for healthy people because they think that, in the worst-case scenario, 'I will think tough, I will think positive, I will fight my way through.' And what about the people who don't make it? My friends in the hospital were doing weird fitness sequences and riding the stationary bike to stay fit to fight cancer. They were the people who did not make it. It feels [like] saying they did not work hard enough."

In his study of the Enterprise Company, Schweingruber touched on this point. "The responsibility for achieving success is placed on individuals," he notes in his report. "Enterprise student dealers are taught that they are responsible for their own success. If they are failing to achieve a certain level of sales, it is assumed that they have not committed to Enterprise thinking and/or are not carrying out prescribed work routines."

So, the supporters of positive thinking get to have it their way no matter what. If people succeed at work, thrive in life, or survive an illness, those supporters can say, "See! It was the positive thinking that did it." But if people don't succeed, don't thrive, or, for the very unfortunate ones, don't survive, supporters of positive thinking can say, "They just didn't think positively enough. If they had, everything would have been okay." Or, even worse, "It was their own doubts and negative thinking that caused their misfortune."

This is perhaps the most significant danger of a simplistic view of positive thinking. To accept that positive thinking is critical to one's success, you'd have to accept the unfortunate implication that people who aren't able to think as positively will tend to fail. That would pass blame onto people who may just be unfortunate or unlucky victims of fate.

The tenacity of this persistent belief probably affects cancer victims more harshly than it does most groups. When Barbara Ehrenreich, the prominent author and columnist, was diagnosed with breast cancer, she combed the Web, books, and magazines for sources of support. She expected to find somewhat saccharine philosophizing about the meaning of life with cancer. But she was surprised to find endless repetitions of statements such as "You caused your cancer and you can cure it!" As she wrote in her book *Bright-Sided*, the more she searched, "the greater my sense of isolation grew . . . I didn't mind dying, but the idea I should do so while clutching a teddy bear and with a sweet little smile on my face—well, no amount of philosophy had prepared me for that."

Of course, it might be worth clutching a teddy bear if the scientific research really shows that this cures cancer. Unfortunately, it doesn't. Much of this research goes something like this: A group of patients are recruited for a study about how the mind affects cancer. Half of them participate in psychotherapy or a support group to help them think positively, and half of them don't. Then the research team patiently waits, noting who dies and who doesn't. Generally, these studies find little or no difference in mortality between the two groups. Depending on the specific type of cancer, about half the people who develop the disease will die; it doesn't seem to make any difference whether they've been coached in positive thinking.

Proponents of the power of positive thinking quickly counter these criticisms by observing that some studies provide evidence that cancer support groups strengthen patients' immune systems. This is true, and it would be a promising finding if it weren't for one thing: A stronger immune system doesn't seem to be very useful for fighting cancer. In some cases, it might even be a *bad* thing, because some tumors enlist the immune system to accelerate growth. Again, psychologist James Coyne, this time joined by his colleagues Howard Tennen and Adelita Ranchor, scrutinized the research that claimed to demonstrate a connection between attending therapy groups and slowing cancer progression. In their 2010 *Annals of Behavioral Medicine* article, they lament, "We examined how unsubstantiated and even implausible the causal links are that are claimed between changes in the measures of immune functioning used in these studies and progression and outcome of cancer. Yet, these claims are directly marketed to cancer patients in press releases from investigators . . . despite careful analysis showing that the interventions are ineffective in affecting recurrence or survival."

This doesn't mean that interventions like these do nothing. Even given these discouraging results, patients still appear to reap substantial *emotional* benefit. Probably the most trumpeted psychological intervention for people with cancer is supportive-expressive therapy, developed by Dr. David Spiegel at Stanford University School of Medicine. As with the other cancer groups we've discussed, the research is far from clear about whether this intervention increases survival. What is much clearer, however, is that group members benefit through improved mood, decreased anxiety, fewer symptoms of traumatic stress, and even reduced perceptions of physical pain. But here's perhaps the most interesting fact about supportive-expressive therapy: it isn't focused merely on increasing positive thinking. Instead, therapists encourage patients to experience and express their thoughts and feelings, *whatever those may be.* In his book *Living Beyond Limits*, Spiegel bears witness to the harrowing conversations that often occur among women with advanced metastatic breast cancer in these groups—conversations about the loss of breasts, the loss of hair, the loss of functioning, and even the loss of life. Although you might think that this experience would be disturbing to the women, Dr. Spiegel observed the exact opposite. Speaking frankly and openly about these difficult topics often makes them less scary.

To avoid them would be simply to deny the reality staring one in the face.

"I don't know what will happen with my eyesight in the future," Alan says he acknowledged after many months of struggle. "I hope my vision won't get worse, but if it does, I want to do everything I can before it's gone." As for his dream of a life in the Royal Navy, he would be dishonest with himself if he didn't admit that it was over. By rejecting simplistic positive thinking, he was truly facing up to the situation. "I know what I can't do now that my eyesight is gone," he said to himself. "So, now I'm going to figure out what I can do."

That's when he came up with the idea to commission a rowboat and paddle from Spain to Barbados. "People thought I was nuts. But this was my life now, and I wanted to do something that stretched me mentally and physically. I was shooting for a watershed moment."

Ironically, it seems that giving up on some dreams—generally not regarded as an act of positive thinking—opened him up to new ones.

At Concordia University, psychologist Carsten Wrosch has spent more than a decade investigating the finer points of giving up. "The notion that persistence is essential for success is deeply embedded within American culture," he writes with coauthor Gregory Miller in the journal *Psychological Science*. But there are times, they argue, when doggedly pursuing a goal may hurt more than it helps. "Specifically, when people find themselves in situations in which they are unlikely to realize a goal, the most adaptive response may be to disengage from it. By withdrawing from a goal that is unattainable, a person can avoid repeated failure experiences and their consequences for mind and body."

That's not merely their opinion. Dozens of studies show that giving up can sometimes be better than persisting. In just one of these studies, Wrosch and his colleagues Jutta Heckhausen and William Fleeson wanted to know how women dealt with a very significant and potentially devastating goal blockage: being unable to have biological children. The goal of having children naturally becomes stymied for all women, of course, sometime between the ages of forty and sixty. This can be a particularly difficult pill to swallow for those who wish they had beaten the deadline. As women without children approach the age of forty, many increase their efforts to become pregnant both through natural as well as medical means. So these researchers administered a battery of questionnaires to 139 women either just before or after the age of forty. They asked whether these women still wanted children and, if so, whether they were actively trying to get pregnant. Most of the women under forty said that one of their major life goals was to have children, and they reported putting a lot of effort into it. The picture changed sharply when the researchers examined the answers of the post-forty-year-old women; only a small minority of them still had a goal to have children. Presumably, realizing that they were most likely past the age at which this goal would be achievable, they had given up trying. This might sound sad. After all, nobody likes the idea of giving up on important goals. But here's why it's not as sad as it seems: the post-age-forty women who lessened the amount of effort invested in the goal of having children felt less depressed than those who continued to invest effort in it. In other words, giving up was associated with better mental health.

Similar beneficial effects of giving up, technically referred to as goal disengagement, have been found for other groups of people as well. It isn't clear exactly why disengagement appears to be beneficial. One possibility is that giving up on some goals frees people to pursue other, previously overlooked ones. There are only so many hours in a day. It makes sense that spending this time on goals that are actually possible given our capabilities and limitations is a better recipe for happiness than yearning for impossible dreams. This doesn't mean lowering one's standards. It simply means beginning the goal pursuit process from where we actually are rather than deluding ourselves or denying the reality of our situation. That's hard to do when we insist on thinking only positive thoughts.

———

Thankfully for Alan, blindness does not affect the physical ability to row. The hardest part of his adventure, in fact, was getting around the boat without bumping into sharp corners or burning himself on the electric stove. Still, there was the very real, very immediate danger of taking a misstep and tumbling overboard, sightless, into the vast expanse below. Even for experienced and fully sighted sailors, the sea is a demanding creature, far from stolid, whose loveliness is entirely fickle.

Alternating between rowing and sleeping, Alan was up two hours before sunrise every day, barreling seawater off the deck, gobbling up energy bars, and checking the oversize GPS for any drift during the night. During his stretch of ten or eleven hours rowing, he listened to music on his iPod while briny-sweet marine water sloshed against the boat and the winds whistled across the hull. At night, the boat drifted on the flat pan of the dark ocean. While Alan couldn't see the stars, he sensed the constellations overhead and filled in the gaps with his mind's eye.

"It was incredibly peaceful, but I was kind of ready for the shit to hit the fan," he says. "You have to be prepared for the worst. The watertight seals could go, which meant we'd take on more water. I was ready for a situation where the boat would be hit by something, or a catastrophic failure of equipment, a bad storm where the boat broke apart, and the worst thing of course: that Matt and I may not survive."

Once again, Alan's thoughts proved realistic. During their fourth evening at sea the ocean turned rough, sending cold water breaching the hull as dark gray swells pummeled the boat. Icy eastern winds pushed the vessel backward toward the tip of Africa, causing Alan and Matt to lose several days' worth of advancement. One by one, the seals broke. Ocean water leaked into the galley, shorting some of the electrical equipment and spoiling their food supplies.

"Like I said," Alan remembers, "it wasn't like I didn't see this coming."

———

When we look at Alan Lock's story of supersurvival alongside that of Maarten van der Weijden, we can see that popular culture's view of positive versus negative thinking fails us. These men embody something more pessimistic than positive thinking yet more realistic than pessimism. Perhaps we can call it true hope or, even better, grounded hope, an approach to life involving building one's choices on a firm understanding of reality. Each started out with a goal that governed his life. Then trauma obstructed that path and set him on another. What makes both their stories of survival special is their ability to stop thinking positively and start thinking realistically, to avoid the comforting fiction that "everything will be fine," and instead bravely to ask, "What now?"

It wasn't as though Alan aspired to be the first blind person to build a rocket ship and fly solo to the moon. That would have been as unrealistic as believing that positive thinking could bring back his eyesight. While traversing three thousand miles of ocean is an outrageous goal, it was something Alan could feasibly do given his talents, drive, and remaining physical abilities. His condition did not impede him. Plus, he took precautions. He considered the real risks and ultimately confronted many of those challenges along the journey. He also confronted the reality of his limitations.

No one is saying that having a good attitude is bad, but the trouble with attributing favorable outcomes to positive thinking is that this can lead to magical thinking and even denial. Believing that an impossible goal such as regaining his eyesight was possible led Alan to misery and frustration. Giving up on that unattainable goal was a prerequisite for true positive thinking—the kind that led him to genuine personal growth. And therein lies the paradox. Giving up is sometimes the only way to move forward. Truly accepting the consequences of a trauma with realistic thinking rather than delusional positive thinking can open people up to true hope—something that enables setting and achieving goals that ultimately can improve one's life.

Let's apply this idea to Maarten. When he was a kid, the people around him told him, uncritically, that he was a world champion swimmer in the making. When he noticed his times were lackluster, he felt that he just wasn't thinking positively enough. All he had to do to win was think good thoughts, and anything was possible. People told him the same thing when he was diagnosed with leukemia, despite the fact that the best science and medical information indicated otherwise. Trying to maintain such positive thinking in the face of obvious contradictory evidence led Maarten to feel exasperated. He knew that if he didn't look reality in the face and admit that the situation was brutally *not* in his favor, he would not have a basis for deciding how to make things better. Much later, he applied this approach to swimming by opting for a realistic view of his capabilities, admitting that many swimmers were naturally more gifted, and setting realistic goals to work around his athletic shortcomings.

And he won the gold—after which he promptly retired from racing. "A lot of Olympic champions go on to compete for many years, but I saw what it would take to maintain that level of commitment. I was training in an altitude tent fifteen hours a day and swimming seven hours a day. If I was honest with myself, that was a reality I no longer wanted. I'd met that goal of becoming a world champion, and it was time to find new goals."

Maarten has since written a book, *Better*, about the myth of positive thinking, that to date has sold close to sixty thousand copies. He also became a manager at Unilever, a large European food and toiletries company. "I noticed that being a hero was not a good atmosphere to accomplish something. When everyone tells you you're so good, you can't improve. Now I talk about laundry products and toothpaste, something I came in knowing nothing about. My hero status disappeared. I set my sight on a new goal, to be the best salesperson I could."

Not surprisingly, Maarten doesn't repeat any scripted positive phrases to boost his sales.

On April 5, 2008, Alan Lock and Matt Boreham reached Barbados in their tiny rowboat exactly eighty-five days, three hours, and twenty minutes after leaving La Gomera to cross the Atlantic Ocean. Most of the watertight seals were worn out. Saltwater had obliterated their reserve of energy bars, nuts, tea, freeze-dried apples, and custards. The portable speakers had fizzled with static and eventually broken altogether. Blisters bloomed on Alan's hands from months of rowing. A constant thrum of pain ratcheted the tightness in his calves. Topping it off, they had run out of chocolate.

They returned to England where Guinness World Records informed Alan that he was the first blind person ever to row any of the world's oceans. This was great news, but Alan hadn't set out to break any records. He was just searching for his watershed moment.

We say that actions are successful when they bring us closer to achieving our goals and unsuccessful when they move us further away from them. We set course to achieve these goals, then muster the will to continue reaching for them. And occasionally we're forced to relinquish one of them. This was true of Alan Lock, who bravely abandoned his past dream, however romantic, of a life of adventure in the Royal Navy, pinned entirely on the return of his vision, and who, in so doing, discovered something new and achievable. While we can't discount the challenges inherent in leaving one path for another, especially when prompted by nothing less than tremendous adversity, it's human nature to strive for what is important to us, just as it was the ocean's nature to tempt Alan to do so.

3

The Truth of Illusion

Don't part with your illusions. When they are gone
you may still exist, but you have ceased to live.
—MARK TWAIN

The greatest way to live with honor in this world is
to be what we pretend to be.
—SOCRATES

Casey Pieretti's right leg has been blown off roughly thirty times
since he became a supersurvivor.

"There was a leg break in *Universal Soldier* and another one in
Priest," says Casey. "In *The Dead Undead*, I got my leg shot off by a
fifty-caliber gun. In *Gamer*, a rocket-propelled grenade." With lazy
exuberance, Casey breezes through the rest of his sizzle reel from the
comfort of his Santa Barbara home, recounting his many wounding
triumphs. He's good-looking and confident on-screen, with a lean,
athletic build; short dark hair smoothly brushed forward; and a bold,
charismatic smile. You might not immediately recognize him, but
odds are you remember one of his mutilations.

In *The Ghost Whisperer*, he broke his leg at the knee. In *The
Shield*, a pit bull shredded it. Jennifer Garner shot it through with
a spear gun in *Alias*. A giant bug even snapped it off completely in

Starship Troopers. When he's not being attacked by vicious dogs and alien insects, he's stunt-driving, rigging huge aerobatics, staging complex fight scenes, and coordinating action sequences. Stunt performers, particularly the good ones, are willing to do it all, risking their lives in the process.

"The way I see it, there's no floor and no ceiling to what I can do. I'm willing to try anything," Casey says. But how many times can he expect to jump onto a moving train or fall from a speeding vehicle before something backfires and he's seriously hurt or even killed?

Take one of his more explicit dismemberments. In director John Woo's World War II–era film, *Windtalkers*, Casey played an American Marine fighting the Imperial Japanese Army during the invasion of Saipan. Having secured the beachhead, his platoon comes under friendly fire. He is running, dodging artillery shells and fiery bomb blasts, when an immense explosion lobs him into the air, chars his face and hands, and obliterates the skin and bones beneath his right knee. The explosion reduces his right leg to a red-and-black charred nub.

The film's production crew had carefully marked off Casey's run, rigged the flash and flares, and set the kerosene and petrol to ignite on cue. When Casey reached his mark, a rig vaulted his body, and he landed on his second mark, all within a single take. Nothing was left to chance. Still, executing these stunts is pretty dangerous work. For every fireball, Casey is dangerously close to actual flames and potential debilitating injury.

He's been near enough to death to know the stakes better than most, both on-and off-screen. Like all supersurvivors, he has faced unexpected peril and narrowly escaped with his life. So how can he so easily take such enormous physical risks for a paycheck? What allows him fearlessly to perform stunts that would petrify almost anyone else?

Sometimes the biggest stunt is convincing yourself there's no risk at all.

Risk is an unavoidable part of life. Virtually all activities, even those that feel safe, involve a certain amount of risk. It's possible that your car could be struck by lightning and collide with oncoming traffic only moments after you leave a restaurant where you contracted salmonella from the lettuce in your sandwich. But most of us assume scenarios like this are pretty unlikely. So, we drive our cars in the rain and eat at the corner diner with little fear. When it comes to skydiving, bungee jumping, or working as a stunt performer, however, we may take a pass, believing that the risk is just a little too great.

Perceptions of risk have real implications for how we behave. A considerable amount of research links people's willingness to engage in a wide array of activities with their perceptions of risk. In general, people who believe that speeding is unsafe drive slower, people who view smoking as unsafe choose not to smoke, and people who consider unprotected sex risky practice safer sex. It's rational, of course, to be more careful when we believe we're at risk. But people's perceptions of risk don't always coincide with reality.

Take texting while driving, for example. To determine the objective danger associated this act, researchers often place people in life-like driving simulators and compare their performance while reading or writing text messages with that when their attention is not divided. The results are startling, with some studies showing that people spend 400 percent more time with their eyes off the road and react to hazards 35 percent slower when sending text messages. In fact, a 2009 study of the driving habits and safety records of a hundred commercial vehicle drivers over a period of eighteen months by the U.S. Department of Transportation found that texting increased the likelihood of accidents and near-accidents by twenty-three times. Texting friends while driving is dangerous; it places us and others at risk, and we shouldn't do it. We probably wouldn't do it if we were good at assessing risk. But it turns out that human beings generally aren't.

Surveys show that up to 73 percent of drivers in the United States at least occasionally send or receive text messages while driving, not to mention 66 percent of drivers in Australia and 62 percent in the United Kingdom. People apparently don't think it's all that risky. In New Zealand, psychologists Charlene Hallett at the University of Auckland and her colleagues Anthony Lambert and Michael Regan recently undertook a national survey in which they asked more than a thousand drivers about their texting perceptions and behaviors. Only 41 percent of respondents said they thought texting while driving was "very unsafe." In fact, 30 percent of respondents said they thought texting while driving was either "very safe" or "moderately safe," while 29 percent said they thought it was only "moderately unsafe." So it shouldn't be surprising that 59 percent of respondents said they regularly received or sent text messages while driving. This doesn't square with the twenty-three-fold increase in objective risk mentioned earlier.

Fortunately, the research also shows that, although notoriously difficult to do, people can shift their perception of risk when they are confronted with the facts. But most of us don't have access to hard data as we go about our day, and in the absence of such data, risk is very much in the eye of the beholder. When someone calls an activity "too risky," it turns out they may be making a statement as much about their own psychology as about the physical world.

———

Though Casey's first public stunt wasn't physically risky, it was a masterpiece of showmanship.

He was a tall, nimble sixteen-year-old, the kind of kid who was both a math whiz and a dynamo on the basketball court. One morning he proved he could be a master of comedy as well, when he graced the school assembly in a dress.

It wasn't the sort of stunt that announces itself with pyrotechnics—he was just showing off—but Casey felt something in the air change when he arrived in the crowded hall. Attention shifted to him. "I don't think most people knew what to think," he recalls. "It was funny—for me, anyway. I learned early on that I liked to expose myself to the admiration or ridicule of my peers by doing or attempting anything and taking big social chances. I found exuberance in nonconformity. People responded to it, so I'd do it more. I'd take on a funny accent for the school play, or do things that were just unexpected." Some might have worried that appearing at a school event in drag would carry harmful academic or social repercussions. But Casey wasn't concerned.

Casey never dreamed that his antics would lead to a future in the daredevil trade of movie aerobatics and television death scenes, or for that matter, catapult him from small-town kid to one of Hollywood's most sought-after stuntmen. Although he never spent much time considering what he would become, he recalls having a sense that he was in control of his future. He could become anything he wanted, and do it—whatever it was—better than anybody. "My attitude's always been I can do anything I set my mind to and do it better than the next guy. I'll fight like hell to prove that to you."

Whether it's his pride or candor, one feels an infectious sense of empowerment when talking to Casey. His message is clear: he succeeded by trying hard and believing he could do anything. But stunt work is a dangerous game. Take the 1998 staged explosion that killed stuntman Marc Akerstream during taping of the series *The Crow: Stairway to Heaven*. Or the case of A. J. Bakunas, who, while performing a three-hundred-foot fall from the Kincaid Towers in Lexington, Kentucky, for the 1979 film *Steel*, tore straight through the soft-landing airbag. (In case you're wondering, the criterion for ensuring 100 percent mortality is a free fall onto a solid surface from the height of ninety to a hundred feet.) Despite safety precautions, accidents in the world of stunt work hurt and kill actors every year.

"You definitely take your life in your own hands when you do this work," Casey says. "I could break my neck, my arms and legs, get burned, or lose a body part." Curiously, even given his open-eyed admission of these dangers, he's pretty certain that these kinds of disasters won't happen to him, otherwise he wouldn't do what he does. When asked about this, he simply grins and says, "But I'm good."

———

Casey clearly believes he's at much lower risk than many people would think they'd be in his position. Some might even call him delusional. But he's hardly alone. More than three decades of research show that such "delusions" are widespread.

Try a little experiment next time you're at a dinner party. Ask people to raise their hands to indicate whether they believe they're at less risk, about equal risk, or greater risk than the average person of just about anything—from having a heart attack to developing cancer to getting into a car wreck to being mugged. Most people will say they're at less risk than average. This is exactly what psychologist Neil Weinstein of Cook College, Rutgers, found in his seminal study published in 1980 in the *Journal of Personality and Social Psychology*. He asked more than two hundred and fifty college students a simple question: "Compared to other Cook students—same sex as you—what are the chances that the following events will happen to you?" Then he listed twenty-four negative events ranging from the merely inconvenient (purchasing a car that turns out to be a lemon) to the catastrophic (developing cancer). For nineteen of the twenty-four events, most students indicated they were at less risk than average. In fact, compared to the few students who thought they were in more danger than the average student, about four times as many estimated that they were safer! This is, of course, statistically impossible. By definition, there should be about equal numbers of people on both sides of the average, with the largest number of people falling just about on the average.

It might be tempting to assume that this phenomenon is limited to idealistic college students who haven't yet been worn down by the realities of life. But the same phenomenon, known as comparative optimism, has been demonstrated in adults and children of all ages in dozens of published studies since Weinstein's paper.

Just like Casey, people generally believe that it—whatever "it" is— won't happen to them.

———

Casey was back in Carson City from his freshman year at Wassuck College, where he had a full scholarship to play basketball. The regulars, his old gang from the class of 1984, were all there that evening in the jet black Oldsmobile 442 that he and his best friend, Kenny, had lovingly rebuilt. With a rev of the restored four-barrel carburetor, the car zigzagged across the highway. As it approached a turn, it took a hard left and fishtailed wildly, righting itself again before gunning forward.

But now smoke was rising from the hood. The boys pulled the car off to the side of the road, where it died.

The driver's-side door opened and Casey stepped out, waving smoke away from his face. Kenny dislodged himself from the passenger side and shouted, "I told you not to take corners with the loose battery!" It had been a raucous night of partying and hitting on girls; Casey had even nearly gotten into a fight. But Casey never drank and drove. Years earlier, his father was driving with Casey's brother when they were struck and killed by a drunk motorist. The loss was devastating to Casey and sent him tumbling into a numbing years-long depression from which he had only recently begun to emerge.

Casey looked down the empty highway and considered their options: wait for help, leave the car and walk to town, try to find a payphone in the middle of nowhere and call a tow truck, or start pushing. Kenny shook his head with bluster. "I'm not leaving the car out here in the middle of nowhere." So Casey decided to push it all the way to Kenny's father's garage, more than two miles, and an hour's march, away. He took a section of the back bumper, and Kenny engaged the clutch. With a mighty heave, the car rolled forward.

Eventually the garage appeared as a miniature reprieve in the distance, its windows and awning dark. A lamppost created a brief respite of light, and beyond that unfurled the unlit expanse of the Sierra Nevada Mountains.

Casey heard what sounded like the grouse of an old engine barreling through the darkness. From behind, a phantom Ford LTD crossed the white line, swerved, and then sped up. The side of the garage swelled with white light. A violent force thundered into Casey from behind. His body was crushed against Kenny's Oldsmobile in a flash of shattering pain. The two vehicles, married by their bumpers, dragged him fifteen yards before releasing him into the darkness of unconsciousness.

"The driver that hit us was drunk," Casey explains mildly. "My right leg two and a half inches below the knee was gone. Both of my knees were turned inside out. My left tibia was crushed. I'd lost a third of the medial gastrocnemius [inner calf] muscle. My left foot was broken but intact."

What were the odds of two drunk drivers, separated by six years, destroying the lives of the Pieretti family? Surely, given the deaths of his father and brother by a drunk driver, Casey realized the risk he was taking by walking along a dark highway accompanied by a pack of teenagers. But just as Neil Weinstein found, on some level Casey believed he was at less risk than average.

Upon waking up in the hospital and facing the long road to physical recovery ahead of him, Casey strangely felt a sense of near-immediate acceptance. "I could have died; I should have died," he says. "But I wasn't dead, and I wasn't willing to waste time. I'd learned to live my life with my father and brother and then to live life without them. It was the same with the leg. I'd had two legs up until age nineteen, and now I was living without one. The core person I was was the same, but what I'd do and choices I'd make had to be radically different."

Within days of the accident, Casey decided that he was going to push through rehab with vigor and run a triathlon in a year. As much as it may seem like it, this wasn't the kind of denial-based positive thinking that Alan Lock and Maarten van der Weijden avoided. Casey was realistically and brutally aware of the cards he had been dealt; there was no denying, ignoring, or distorting the absence of a leg. He fully understood the difficulties that awaited him, and he was prepared to confront every one. "Most people would say 'never,' but I just knew I could do it and be the best I could be, and I'd be relentless at going after it, too." To his credit, almost a year to the day after his accident, Casey strapped on a carbon-fiber energy-storing prosthetic and ran a mile in seven minutes. He was racing competitively within the next year—no easy task for someone with two perfectly workable legs, let alone the survivor of major trauma. Friends found Casey's unapologetic confidence in his ability to rebuild his life at best admirable and at worst the result of delusion.

Turns out it was both.

—————

Many factors influence people's perceptions of risk, but perhaps the most powerful one is a sense of personal control, something Casey has in spades. People who feel more in control of outcomes in their lives believe they're at less risk than those who feel less in control. In that study of students at Cook College, Neil Weinstein sought to discover not only whether comparative optimism existed, but also what factors might make it more likely to occur. So he asked research participants to indicate their perceptions of a number of factors he thought might be associated with greater comparative optimism, including the perceived probability of the negative events, people's past experience with similar events, and how desirable they thought it was to avoid such events. People's perception that they could control the events was more strongly related to their degree of comparative optimism than any of these factors. Of the many factors investigated in the three decades since Weinstein's paper, only the stereotype-driven belief that "this kind of event happens only to a certain kind of person"—people of color, overweight people, old people—seems to be a more powerful predictor of whether people will unrealistically underestimate their own risk.

University of California–Los Angeles psychologist Shelley Taylor coined the term *positive illusion* to refer to the overestimation of personal control and similarly overblown views of the self. In fact, she and her colleagues have produced more than two decades' worth of research showing that the vast majority of people carry around such illusions. At first it may seem that she's saying nearly everyone is delusional. So it's important to understand that this isn't exactly what she means. Delusions are extreme misperceptions of reality. People with intense forms of schizophrenia, for instance, may believe they're the reincarnation of Jesus, are transmitting their thoughts to the television news anchor, are working as secret government spies, or, alternatively, are being monitored by secret government spies. These gross misconstructions are sharply detrimental to normal functioning, often destroying jobs, straining relationships, and necessitating hospitalization. In contrast, Taylor and coauthor David Armor write in the *Journal of Personality* that positive illusions are people's "mildly distorted positive perceptions of themselves (self-aggrandizement), an exaggerated sense of personal control, and overly optimistic expectations about the future." We're not talking about "crazy" here; we're talking about confident.

So far we've argued that having such positive illusions, particularly the overestimation of one's degree of control, is associated with taking risks. Although being willing to assume such risks helped turn Casey into one's of Hollywood's most lauded stuntmen, surely he is the exception. Overconfidence in one's ability to control situations is bad for the rest of us, right? Surprisingly, in many cases, the science is beginning to show just the opposite.

In the 1970s, as a doctoral student studying organizational behavior at UCLA, Marshall Goldsmith began to notice that certain characteristics and behavior patterns were common among extremely successful people. During the thirty-five years since, Goldsmith has devoted thousands of hours to executives from some of the world's largest and most influential companies, attempting to understand the qualities that breed success. He's had dinner with them and spent time in their boardrooms, private offices, and homes. Early on, he noticed something odd.

"These successful people are all delusional!" he says, but cautions, "This is not to be misinterpreted as a bad thing. In fact, being delusional helps us become more effective. By definition, these delusions don't have to be accurate. If they were totally accurate, your goals would be too low."

Goldsmith noticed that although illusions of control expose people to risk of failure, they do something else that is very interesting: they motivate people to keep trying even *when* they've failed. "If we have the illusion that we're great, we're open to trying more things," Goldsmith insists. "Successful people fail a lot, but they try a lot, too. When things don't work, they move on until an idea does work. Survivors and great entrepreneurs have this in common."

This sureness in people's ability to control their own destinies can come across as a lack of humility. Goldsmith cautions that it's not narcissism, however, even though it may look like it from a distance. "It's actually self-confidence. The single strongest thread of commonality between mega-successful business executives is self-confidence. In my experience, zero CEOs have low self-confidence, and no top executives from multibillion-dollar corporations have low self-confidence, either."

In supersurvivors, too, we see that illusions of control may be a key to extraordinary accomplishments. The perception of control permits people to take all kinds of risks. It even informs what types of risks they take. Dropping everything to riskily pursue rock stardom, Asha Mevlana needed such illusions. So did Alan Lock, as he strove to become the first blind person to row across the Atlantic Ocean. From this perspective, most supersurvivors we interviewed strongly believed that they had both the right and the personal capability to do what they'd done. Just as Goldsmith observed of mega-rich CEOs, positive illusions seem to increase supersurvivors' chances of success. Without the basic belief that they have control over their destinies despite ample evidence to the contrary, these people might not have become supersurvivors at all.

According to Goldsmith, successful people believe that they have the internal capacity to make desirable things happen. "People who believe they can succeed see opportunities where others see threats," he explains. "To put it simply—they try more different things."

It's reasonable to question what seems to be a contradiction here. In chapter 2 we told you that positive thinking can be dangerous, and now it seems we're saying just the opposite. For this reason, it's important to contrast these productive positive illusions of control with the denial-based positive thinking we previously argued could be damaging. In her *Journal of Personality* article, Shelly Taylor directly addresses this issue. "On the surface, positive illusions may look like mind-numbing bromides that get people through trying situations by permitting them to ignore the objective evidence and to maintain a fictional belief akin to denial that all will be well if one takes no action and waits things out," she writes. But whereas denial-based positive thinking is a distortion of the *situation*, positive illusions are slightly inflated views of *oneself* and one's ability to control one's future. Denying or distorting a bad situation may be comforting in the short term, but it's potentially harmful in the long run because it will be almost impossible to solve a problem unless you first admit you have one. In contrast, having an especially strong belief in one's personal capabilities, even if that belief is somewhat illusory, probably *helps* you to solve problems. Casey didn't expect a car to hit him that night, but it did. Yet he still believed he was in control of his own destiny—even if he couldn't control the things that happened to him, he could certainly control what he *did with those events* through his own actions.

What we're talking about here is the same kind of grounded hope we advocate in chapter 2, but now we're getting more specific. A useful, if somewhat simplistic, mathematical formula might be: a realistic view of the situation + a strong view of one's ability to control one's destiny through one's efforts = grounded hope. Dozens of studies have shown that hope predicts all kinds of positive outcomes, including success in athletics, better college grades, better mental and physical health, a greater sense of meaning in life, and even better psychotherapy outcomes.

In one study, David Feldman (one of the authors of this book), along with his colleagues Kevin Rand and Kristin Kahle-Wrobleski, asked more than a hundred and fifty college students at the beginning of the spring semester to name seven goals they wanted to achieve by the end of the academic year. Not surprisingly, students' aspirations varied widely, encompassing everything from "get a 3.0 GPA" and "get rid of my love handles" to "raise an additional $10,000 for our United Nations Association chapter" and "dedicate more time in my life to God to understand my path on earth." The study set out to determine if it was possible to predict who would make the most progress toward accomplishing their goals by the end of the semester, a challenging task without a crystal ball. Three months later, as the end of the semester neared, students were invited back to report on their progress. On average, students with higher hope at the beginning of the semester were further along on all seven goals than those with lower hope.

This may be because the high-hope students put more effort into pursuing their goals and tried more things, particularly when faced with setbacks. Hopeful thinkers tend to use more problem-focused coping, such as gathering information about a problem, seeking practical assistance from others, and taking action. Arizona State

University researchers Natalie Eggum, Julie Sallquist, and Nancy Eisenberg provided evidence for this. With the help of translators, they interviewed fifty-two adolescents who lived in rural areas near Tororo, Uganda, to investigate the connection between hopeful thinking and coping with adversity. It's not hard to find adversity in Uganda, where things such as poverty, violence, and the loss of parents to AIDS are parts of kids' daily lives. In fact, at an average age of thirteen, 21 percent of the kids had already lost a parent, 63 percent didn't have enough food to eat, and 56 percent had witnessed violence. For many of the children, problems came in groups. "It was very difficult when my father died. I thought I was going to even leave school," one boy explained. "No way we can get even food. Even our mummy did not have work or a way to get a job." According to the results, the kids who tested higher in hope tended to practice higher levels of a variety of coping strategies, but most relevant, they reported engaging in proactive, problem-oriented coping. In contrast to dwelling on their admittedly dire situations, they reported *doing* things to comfort themselves and improve their lives. As some of the children explained, "Instead of being annoyed, I can go to my books and be happy"; "I study and if I get good marks, then I feel better"; and "If I have planted crops, I check on them."

It is in this tendency toward *doing* that grounded hope may help create a better existence for those who practice it. If other people were faced with the daily traumas and tragedies of these Ugandan youth, they might consider it more rational to give up. The situation seems reminiscent of the myth of Sisyphus, who was condemned by the gods to push a boulder again and again up a mountain, only to see it roll back down to the bottom. What's the use?

Perhaps these Ugandan adolescents know something we don't. Maybe they're teaching us a lesson about the utility of believing that, in the face of all contrary evidence, something better is possible. In fact, such hope seems to mitigate the negative effects of trauma. When University of South Carolina psychologist Kerrie Glass and her colleagues interviewed 228 adult survivors of Hurricane Katrina, they found that people with higher levels of hope had lower levels of distress and fewer symptoms of posttraumatic stress disorder. Similarly, when David Berendes, Francis Keefe, and their colleagues at Duke University Medical Center surveyed 51 patients with lung cancer, they found that people with greater levels of hope tended to have less depression and fewer physical symptoms such as pain, fatigue, and cough, regardless of the severity of their cancers.

The stories of supersurvivors vary dramatically from person to person, and yet we see time and again their sense of grounded hope. They seem to come to a place where they are willing to try more things, and to try different things, than they ever have before. The catalyst was a trauma, but an important part of the method for supersurviving is an unusual assessment of risk driven by an abiding belief that, through their own personal efforts, they control their own destinies. Even though their belief in their personal control may seem unwarranted to casual observers, in an interesting sort of self-fulfilling prophesy, it seems to create the conditions for a better future.

———

Four years after the accident that robbed Casey of his limb and nearly his life, he stood once again on the side of a highway. Gray clouds and rain added peril to Interstate 101's car-choked morning commute. Dressed in reflective gear, Casey tightened the buckles of his skates and secured the suspension system that latched his artificial leg to his body. He stomped the wheels of his right in-line skate on the pavement to be sure it was securely attached to his prosthesis. The rain brought oils to the surface of the concrete, slicking the ground. He'd need to factor this into the journey. After the first mile, he was able to tune out the click-clack click-clack of his strides. The stunt was supposed to be skating three thousand miles from San Diego to Washington DC, but the real stunt was not getting squashed by cars, staying hydrated, treating sun exposure, and making it across the country in one piece.

Modern prosthetic limbs are near-miraculous devices that often afford people a life without significant impediment or compromise. Made of carbon-fiber pylon with a suspension systems of straps, belts, sleeves, and airtight seals to keep them attached, they've gotten lighter, more advanced, and more controllable over the years.

Casey was fitted with his first artificial leg almost immediately after the accident. Just months earlier, he had been an ambitious athlete with a full ride to Nevada's Wassuck College to play basketball. Now he'd lost that scholarship and had transferred to the University of California–Santa Barbara. To help pay for school, he took a job as a coat checker at a nightclub. The regular bouncer didn't show up one night, so Casey offered to step in.

Most people in his position might not have volunteered for the job, believing that a one-legged bouncer would not exactly strike fear into the hearts of would-be troublemakers. But Casey is not most people. Unfortunately, the owner of the club refused to give him the job. "[He] questioned my ability to do it. From the moment I lost my leg, I was told what I *couldn't* do," Casey says with indignation in his voice. "On the one hand, sure, to try and pick up where I left off before the accident was idealistic but impossible. But I was still the same core person, and this was discrimination plain and simple."

But what could Casey do about it? Driven by the same over-the-top belief in his ability to control his life through his own efforts, Casey was certain that there were things he could do that people with two legs couldn't or simply wouldn't. "I'm going to do one thing that will show everyone in the world what I am capable of, and no one will ever tell me again what I can or can't do," he decided. It would have to be something outrageous and very different from anything he'd ever done before. Exactly what that big and bold thing would be remained elusive until happenstance stepped in, a chance encounter that Casey would masterfully parlay into opportunity.

In 1987 he was on a flight to Miami when he found himself seated next to another amputee. "I couldn't believe it. He was the exact same size as me, only he was missing his left leg, not his right," Casey says. The guy was part of the U.S. ski team, and Rollerblade was sponsoring him. Of course, with one leg, he used only one skate, and now he offered the unused one to Casey. The in-line skate would later come in handy for getting across UC Santa Barbara's sprawling thousand-acre campus, a beautiful yet time-consuming terrain for Casey.

The peculiar sight of a one-legged student in-line skating across university grounds quickly caught the attention of a girl on the school's stunt skating demo team. "Why aren't you on two skates?" she asked.

"The problem was my prosthetic leg wouldn't stay in a skate very well," Casey remembers. "This very nice girl made a call and got me a matching skate. I took it and cut it up, pulled out the weights, and made it lighter. My foot didn't exactly fit, so I customized the prosthesis." At age twenty-four, he joined that charitable girl on Team Rollerblade, an aggressive in-line skating stunt troupe.

It was here, as Casey's confidence grew, that he found *the idea* that would once and for all convince people what he was capable of. "I met a guy named Joel Bott at a charity skating event. He had the crazy idea to skate across the country," Casey says. "Along the way, we'd raise awareness and funds for a limb bank for amputee kids, who could use reconditioned prostheses other kids had outgrown." The idea took flight, and in the spring of 1993, Joel and Casey launched the Blade Across America tour. "I was confident at this point that I'd wind up back on top," he says, and his belief in his own ability to affect the situation only grew as he secured sponsors and private donors for his cross-country trip.

The Blade Across America tour started with great fanfare and media attention from Mission Beach, San Diego. From here, the duo skated the dusky desert highway from California into the low, reddish mountains of the Southwest in fifty-mile stretches. A lot can happen in fifty miles. Deserts turn into cities, cities into subdivisions. Every new place has its own vibrant character. Casey skated past seemingly endless stretches of mini-malls and billboards, gas stations, housing projects, tract homes, steel buildings, factories, schools, graveyards, and churches. Pavement turned to gravel, to sand, to mud and tar. Ruddy skies transitioned to gray, deep blues, rich purples, tungsten, and obsidian.

Beginning in New Mexico, the two set up ramps and presented three stunt shows a night at Veterans Affairs hospitals, school parking lots, and skate shops, performing tricks, jumping barriers, and hurling themselves over reporters, cars, and spectators to the pleasure of the grandstands. The crowds responded with cheers as Casey contorted his body in the air, turned, and gained speed, displaying complete control and mastery of his skill.

Of course, he wasn't always masterful.

At a skate show in Texas, an exhausted Casey was ad-libbing a stunt, missed the ramp with one skate, and hit the audience member he was jumping over. Later, in Richmond, Virginia, as he was jumping over a Cadillac, his prosthetic leg came off in midflight, causing him to crash to the ground, separate his shoulder, and tear up the right side of his body. His injuries were serious enough that his doctor told him to stop skating.

Undeterred, in the morning, Casey squeezed into his skates and harnesses, ate a power bar, and returned to the road. With one arm now in a sling, he skated on to Mount Vernon in ninety-five-degree heat, just a bit wobblier than the day before.

Applying the formula for grounded hope, it's easy to see what kept Casey going. Although he had a brutally realistic understanding of the trials and tribulations of his journey and of the difficulties of making it on a prosthetic leg, his belief in his ability, through his own efforts, to make the best of that journey never wavered. With this combination of a realistic understanding of the situation and confidence in your ability to face it, there's always a reasons to keep trying to solve whatever difficulties life throws at you.

The Blade Across America tour left Casey with a nickname among peers and fans. "People called me a 'super-cripple.' It's a funny name, but it's sort of true," he concedes. The problem, as critics have pointed out, is that focusing on the exceptional triumphs of a few capable disabled people, or "super-cripples," obscures the day-to-day needs of the disabled majority. "But I liked to think I was doing some good with this stunt," Casey says. "It started out as a way to prove I could do anything on one leg as well, if not better, than someone with two legs, but it became something else in the end." In June of 1993, Casey addressed Congress and met with Senator Ted Kennedy to draw media attention to the needs of amputee children whose families couldn't afford to replace their prostheses as their kids grew. Perhaps his greatest stunt yet, Casey's three-thousand-mile journey in eighty-nine days led to the development of the National Limb Bank. Casey was also responsible for raising tens of thousands of dollars for education, research, and rehabilitation.

Back home in Santa Barbara, he continued to skate professionally for a couple of years. He took acting classes on the side, got his Screen Actors Guild card, and auditioned for some small roles in film and commercials. In 1991 agents started calling. There was even some buzz about turning Casey's story into a movie. Though such a film never materialized, he liked Hollywood. From stunt skater to stuntman was a natural leap. He trained to do high falls, stair tumbles, and fight scenes; to throw a punch, sell a shot, handle weapons, and master a sword. "I know I take life in my own hands every time I do a stunt," he says. "But you have the knack or you don't. Most people would never say, 'I could be a stuntman,' so they don't try. But I just knew I could do it and be the best at it. I was relentless at pursuing it."

We've heard these types of survivor stories before. Unexpected tragedy greets an unassuming guy, destroys his life, and he struggles to regain a normal, reasonably well-adjusted existence, ultimately becoming more than he ever dreamed possible. Casey has now appeared in more than fifty films and television series. He's currently working with the biggest action film directors, including Paul Verhoeven, Sam Raimi, and Steven Spielberg.

But looking at Casey Pieretti through the prism of positive illusions and the hope they afford, we know that there's much more to his narrative than his casual metamorphosis might lead people to believe. Casey is, after all, only human. He would be a successful stuntman only if he were capable of reaching his goals based on realistic limitations. But the science shows that this goal pursuit process is at least partly dependent on a sense of control and self-confidence. Unfortunately, the nature of trauma is that it so easily rips these away. It strips the soul of its strength and overtakes our perception of safety, replacing it with fear. Casey's overly positive faith in his ability to control his environment seems to have protected him from this eventuality, leading him through two traumas to supersurvivorship.

Exaggerated perceptions of control can open people up to taking risks. If your purpose in life is to avoid danger at all costs, such exposure to risk is bad. But a completely risk-avoidant existence also forecloses opportunity. In many cases, when it comes to bouncing forward after a trauma and doing great things, it may take a bit of overconfidence and a slightly skewed perception of risk. Many of us are "smart" and never attempt half the crazy things supersurvivors do. But we also never achieve their elevated successes, even though we might be perfectly capable of it.

In April of 2009, Casey was struck by another big idea. Along with the stunt work, he had established his own company, AMP'D Gear, to promote the ingenuity of amputees in sports. Looking to take this business concept to the next level, he pitched a concept for a documentary television show in which he created prostheses for all kinds of extreme sports. Intrigued, a producer asked to see a tape. Casey made a short reel, and eight months later the pilot for *Bionic Builders* aired. "Only once, and that's it," Casey says. "We were late turning in episodes, we were over budget, and our executive producer left. The show was canceled." As Marshal Goldsmith discovered, however, the most successful people try many different things. Casey is now pitching a repackaged version of the show for Spike TV. It's a smarter show, he says, "more motivational and transformative." Casey knows full well that the first attempt was a failure, but he also is absolutely sure the next one will succeed.

This may seem delusional—until, like so many things in Casey's life, overconfidence and persistence make it happen.

4

The World We Thought We Knew

It was completely fruitless to quarrel with the world.
—SØREN KIERKEGAARD

Mother's Day 2003 would be forever fixed in Paul Rieckhoff's memory as the day he became a killer for a cause he didn't understand. The U.S. Army First Brigade, Third Infantry, was stationed in Baghdad's converted Medical City complex. At six feet two with a low, intense stare and a head shaven smooth as a boulder, Paul, the platoon's leader, was an imposing guy. It's hard to imagine that anyone would be stupid enough to pick a fight with him, even a gunfight. When the enemy started shelling, Paul sprang into action. After running to the front of the building and taking cover behind a retaining wall, he angled his rifle and squinted through the scope, scanning the city. From this high vantage point, he could see past downtown buildings all the way to the banks of the Tigris River. There was movement under the base of a small bridge two hundred meters away. He took two quick breaths, aimed, and squeezed his trigger.

Paul's grandfather fought in World War II, and his father served in Vietnam. Given this proud history, Paul had good reasons to enlist. But by the time he found himself in Iraq, these reasons seemed a faded memory. Four years earlier, he had just graduated from Amherst

College with six-figure job offers in hand. But he turned them all down to join the army. He carried an unusually strong burden of privilege. His gratitude for a life of prosperity fueled a strong desire to give back to the country that had given him so much.

"People didn't think much about patriotism, especially not in the liberal collegiate well-heeled part of Western Massachusetts where I went to college," he writes in his 2006 memoir, *Chasing Ghosts*. "But that's why I wanted to join. I loved my country. I had been afforded tremendous opportunities in this country and I wanted to give something back." Since childhood, Paul had believed in the ideal of the noble warrior fighting bravely for what was good and right. He also fantasized about being the ultimate American badass. So in January of 1999 he arrived at Fort McClellan, Alabama, for basic training. Shortly thereafter, he enrolled in Officer Candidate School, got his commission, and joined the infantry. It was peacetime, but when bad people did bad things in the world, Paul hungered to be part of the solution. It's what he calls his social accountability to a nation that had given him and his family so much. It was his duty to serve his country and the just principles for which he was sure it stood. So, in the spring of 2003, Paul didn't hesitate when he was tapped to become part of Operation Iraqi Freedom, the mission to strip an "Axis of Evil" nation of its weapons of mass destruction and make the world safer.

His platoon was stationed in Kuwait. Paul was awaiting orders to deploy to Baghdad when President George W. Bush announced aboard the USS *Abraham Lincoln*, beneath a banner reading "Mission Accomplished," that Operation Iraqi Freedom had been a success. Apparently the war was over, and Paul had missed it.

So it seemed strange to him that, the very same day, his platoon was ordered to Baghdad. Paul expected to arrive in a newly liberated country, one whose grateful citizens would greet his platoon with open arms, as the architects of Operation Iraqi Freedom had promised. What he found, however, was a disorganized American military facing a very dangerous situation.

There were too few vehicles, not enough ammunition, and a shortage of medical supplies. Many days, Paul's platoon patrolled the streets of Baghdad in one hundred and twenty-degree heat with only a single bottle of water per soldier. His men lacked crucial body armor, which left them to dodge bullets in Vietnam-era flak vests. The constant shootings, killings, kidnappings, and robberies took their toll. Paul's platoon waited endlessly for U.S. and allied troops to fill the city and for military police to line the streets, for foreign aid to arrive, for interpreters to show up, and for supply lines to get fixed. From Paul's perspective, the army had done too little to prepare him and his fellow soldiers for the realities on the ground, and a lack of government planning had set them up for failure.

The mission had clearly not been accomplished. In fact, it was only getting started.

Enduring the Mother's Day battle at the Tigris River and the dozens of other attacks he survived left Paul's world shaken. Upon returning home, he was diagnosed with the nightmares and flashbacks so common to posttraumatic stress disorder. Though these acute psychological wounds would heal with time, a more long-lasting one would remain: Paul began to question his most precious beliefs about duty, justice, and the values for which his country stood. "What they didn't tell you was just how hard it is to come back," he says.

———

In previous chapters, we examine the importance of realistic thinking to finding real hope. In this chapter, we look beyond hope and to a certain type of faith, the kind we experience every day in our lives. When we think of faith, spiritual and religious convictions naturally come to mind. We know it takes faith to believe in God, but we sometimes forget how much faith it takes to believe in truth, justice, goodness, and even love. Trauma challenges this faith, and in some cases shatters it into tiny pieces. We are left groping around on the floor for the ruins of our once-unquestioned beliefs.

Even the most jaded people carry around some pretty benevolent assumptions about the way the world works. Research by University of Massachusetts psychology professor Ronnie Janoff-Bulman suggests that, on some unspoken level, most people believe three important assumptions: that the world is basically good, that good things happen to good people, and that they, fortunately, are good people. Collectively, she refers to these three beliefs as our *assumptive worldview.*

It's easy to doubt Janoff-Bulman's theory. "After all," many people respond, "I read the newspaper. I know the world isn't always a good place." True, on a conscious level, at least. Nonetheless, Janoff-Bulman makes the case that most of us *act* as though these assumptions were true even if we superficially deny them. And actions speak louder than words.

Despite what we see in the newspaper about crimes, victimizations, assaults, and even terrorist attacks, we leave our houses every day without fear. We jump in large steel deathtraps and hurtle ourselves down hard cement highways surrounded by other steel deathtraps. We even speed. In many cities, motorcycles with exposed and often unhelmeted riders zoom between cars, riding painted dividing lines, inches from vehicles to their right and left, the riders apparently oblivious to the very real risk of death or paralysis. It's even common for otherwise upstanding citizens to have a couple glasses of wine or a few beers then casually jump behind the wheel and *assume* that everything will be fine. Don't they know the statistics about drinking and driving? Don't they read the newspaper? Don't they know the law?

Of course they do. But they assume *it won't happen to them.* Most people know superficially this isn't right. But on a deeper level, we are genuinely surprised when something bad happens to someone whom we know to be good. Whenever a dear loved one dies, someone asks, "How could this happen to such a good person?" This isn't denial;

they're genuinely perplexed because, deep down, most of us believe in Janoff-Bulman's assumptive worldview

Most of the time, it's healthy for us to believe that the world is good, that good things happen to good people, and that we are good people. These beliefs help us function well, avert fear, and live happy lives in a world that could otherwise be pretty scary. Could you imagine how terrible life would seem if we thought the opposite—that the world is dangerous, that bad things can as easily happen to good people as bad people, and that we are not good people? So, the brain fights hard to maintain these assumptions.

According to classic research by psychologist Melvin Lerner, our need to maintain our rosy worldview, particularly our belief in a just world, is one of the major causes of victim blaming. The logic goes something like this: When we hear that something terrible has happened to someone, this presents a challenge to our most basic assumptions about fairness. It forces us to doubt that the world is good and just. We may start to wonder if we could fall victim to a rape, assault, robbery, or attack just like that person. So, to comfort ourselves and maintain our sense of safety, we psychologically separate ourselves from the victim. The victim must have *done something* to invite the tragedy. That rape victim must have been wearing provocative clothing. That robbery victim must have been stupid enough to be in the wrong part of town. That assault victim must have been associating with the wrong people. Maybe she was trying to buy drugs at the time. Maybe he was doing something else illicit. Surely these victims were bad people or at least were doing something bad; that's why something bad happened to them—and, so the logic goes, that's why it *won't* happen to me. I'm a good person.

Obviously, this self-deceptive strategy works only when the trauma hasn't happened to us. But even if we are the victims, we may still try desperately to maintain our worldview. That's because it contains our most cherished beliefs and values, most of which fall into Janoff-Bulman's three assumptive worldview categories, which encompass our beliefs about duty, God, decency, friendship, and just about everything else.

Deep patriotism was an important part of Paul's worldview. "It's patriotism in the old-school sense of the word," he says. "It's understated, subtle, a sense of loyalty that's to be expected in every American, the way my grandparents were patriotic. They were immigrants. There was no question of proving your patriotism back then. It was a different kind of social accountability. They gave me an appreciation for what this country has, and it greatly shaped my point of view and my worldview."

He truly believed in the values that most American schoolchildren are taught their country stands for. To Paul, the United States sought to reward and to strengthen democracy and human rights. It used its military might only for the purpose of bolstering those values and justly punishing those who violated them. All it asked in return for this great service was its citizens' faith and obedience. And Paul took his part seriously, forgoing personal gain to join the military.

But what happens when the other end of the bargain isn't upheld, when we begin to realize that our worldview may not be accurate?

———

Adam Savage is a kind of expert in questioning people's assumptions. He is a host of the Discovery television series *MythBusters*, and it's his business to disassemble and apply scientific pressure to the world's most deeply ingrained urban legends and popular lore. Can a cocktail of Diet Coke and Mentos make your stomach explode? Can plugging your finger into the barrel of a gun cause the weapon to backfire? Can cell phone usage really cause a gas station to blow up? For more than ten seasons to date, *MythBusters* has put seven hundred–plus such beliefs to the test.

In one of its most infamous episodes, the show tested a hypothesis that was the subject of contentious debate. The question goes something like this: Imagine that an airplane sits atop a large conveyer belt instead of a runway. The plane begins to move in one direction while the conveyor belt moves in the opposite direction, its speed matched perfectly to that of the aircraft. Can the plane actually take off?

"It's one of those weird things. Both sides of the physics argument adamantly stand by their theory. Some say no plane on a conveyor belt can take off if the speeds are matching in opposite directions. The other side says the plane will take off," says Savage from his studio in San Francisco.

This might not seem like a hot-button issue to you, but it has become just that for thousands of people. Numerous websites have hosted vitriolic conversations devoted to this question. So, in 2008, *MythBusters* rigged a massive conveyor belt and maneuvered a four-hundred-pound ultralight plane onto the makeshift airstrip. "Most of the time the show has at least an idea how an experiment will turn out," Savage says. "In this case, we were equally divided. We had no idea what would happen."

With the two mechanisms perfectly synchronized, the pilot started the plane. The propeller whirred. The ultralight plane accelerated and, to many people's surprise and chagrin, lifted effortlessly into the sky. Here's why: Unlike with, say, a car on a conveyor belt, an airplane's thrust acts upon the air, not the ground. It's a simple, clear answer supported by a simple, clear empirical test.

But a funny thing happened. "We did not change a single person's mind," says Savage. A typical *MythBusters* episode gets ten pages of viewer comments on the Discovery Channel website. For this episode, however, they received six hundred pages. "A thousand people immediately jumped online maintaining a plane rigged to a reverse conveyor belt at linked speeds would result in the plane just sitting there. Our evidence was absolutely clear. But people still got intensely argumentative. They were looking for flaws in experimental setup and our methodology. We still get notes and letters with people refusing to believe it."

The show's executive producer, Dan Tapster, has a theory about why. "People hold on to certain ideas for so long and so absolutely that even in the face of irrefutable proof to the contrary, it's easier to think the evidence is wrong instead of thinking they were wrong the whole time," he says.

Or, as Adam Savage succinctly puts it, people are stubborn. "They hold on to preconceptions. It's a basic human thing. We do have the ability to have our minds changed, but why do it when the burden of proof is always on the disbelievers?"

Urban legends are a lot of fun, but they rarely have real-world consequences beyond the speculative. Life as we know it is not going to end if a commonly held belief is suddenly dispelled.

But what if it actually did?

We can think of our assumptive worldview as a kind of personal myth, only this myth has weight and potentially devastating consequences attached to it. If a myth about an airplane on a runway causes this much upheaval, imagine what might happen if a myth were affixed with real-world weight—say, everything you believed about yourself, your country, and even the world. In this scenario, there's no online forum and nobody to debate with. There's just you.

———

Paul was standing on an airstrip at New York's LaGuardia Airport, there to test his own personal myth. LaGuardia was a world away from the American-occupied Saddam Hussein International Airport and free of bullet-riddled terminals and bombed-out Iraqi tanks.

An official presidential campaign plane touched down in the distance. As it taxied in, Secret Service agents began looking busy around Paul. A handler placed Paul at the end of a row of veterans from different wars, who stood like a living timeline of service to a country supposedly worth dying for.

Three months prior, Paul had returned to the United States from Iraq a changed man. In the war, he'd seen men fatally wounded, a parade of victims carried in and out of Baghdad hospitals, even a squad leader who'd lost both his legs. Thankfully, all thirty-nine men in Paul's platoon had come home alive, though six hundred other soldiers at this point in the war had not.

Back at home, Paul reconnected with his girlfriend and tried to settle back into life as he'd known it before the war. But some things still troubled him, kept him up at night, and ate at him from the inside. "I had problems with the way the U.S. fought the war," he says. "There were never enough troops on the ground. Officers and soldiers in the field were being deployed with no training in Iraqi culture and customs. They received little direction from above, and were vulnerable to attacks. Far more troops were dying in the peacekeeping phase than had been killed during the invasion and defeat of Saddam's military. I was certain about my assessment of the war. I knew that it was the wrong battle, fought at the wrong time, for the wrong reasons."

He'd gone to Iraq to fight for justice and to hold bad people responsible for their misdeeds. It all seemed clear enough, at first: the U.S. soldiers were the good guys; the ones fighting for Saddam's dying regime were the bad guys. Only, by this time, Paul realized that the good guys had sent him to fight under erroneous, even false pretenses. All this challenged his notions that the world was basically safe, that good things happened to good people, and that his country stood for those good things and good people.

Paul decided he had to set things right. It was an election year, and he thought that both parties were equally poorly informed about the realities of the war. Though it was a long shot, he reached out to the Bush and Kerry presidential campaigns, offering his services to set the record straight. To an outsider, this might have seemed like an audacious, bigheaded move. But Paul had always been a confident guy; some might even say he had the advantage of the positive illusions of control discussed in chapter 3. This confidence paid off when a Vietnam vet from New York who worked for John Kerry's campaign returned Paul's call. "He asked if I'd like to meet the senator," Paul recalls. "He felt that Kerry, a war vet himself, should meet guys like me who had actually served in the war." Paul's a smart guy. He knew this would be little more than a photo op for the senator. Still, he wasn't about to pass up this opportunity.

Now, on the LaGuardia tarmac, Senator Kerry, tall and lean, the Democratic nominee for president, emerged from the plane's passenger compartment. Paul had never met a senator before, let alone a presidential candidate, and he was nervous. As Kerry proceeded down the row of veterans, stopping for handshakes and photographs, Paul straightened his back and drew in a breath of air. Kerry approached, noted that Paul was an Iraq War vet, and asked him simply, "How is it?"

Paul started in on a methodical, impassioned response. "I wanted this man to know that my guys and thousands like them had gotten screwed. I wanted him to know that America was not better off as a result of the Iraq War. I wanted him to know the truth about Iraq from a man who had served. I wanted him to understand why the war was keeping me up at night. I wanted him to feel the urgency. And I wanted him to tell the world." Despite his conscious statements to the contrary, on some very real level, Paul believed Kerry would listen. Perhaps his words would trigger the senator's personal sense of social accountability—his own values of duty and justice. Maybe then the world would return to normal.

The senator stood silently and responded with little more than a favorable nod. Much to Paul's surprise, however, several days after this brief meeting, the Kerry campaign called. The president was going to be giving an address on the anniversary of his now-infamous "Mission Accomplished" speech. The Kerry campaign wanted Paul to give the formal rebuttal directly after the address. The speech would catapult Paul onto the national stage. He was used to taking fire, but this was going to put him in the crosshairs of the national political machine.

His stomach hurt. Yet Senator Kerry had answered his call for social accountability. Paul gave the address.

The next day, national television and radio were all over him. "People said I was the voice of dissent on the Iraq War. They said I might be the next John Kerry," writes Paul. "The next John Kerry? A week ago I had been an ordinary guy just back from Iraq, sitting across from a hairy, fat blackjack dealer named Chi Chi, debating whether to split a pair of fours. Now people were calling me a hero or a traitor." And he was just getting started.

———

At first blush, Paul seems to have dramatically changed his views of his country. After all, this once-stalwart soldier suddenly became a rebel. Many of his closest friends were mystified by the transformation. People who didn't know him were quick to brand him a traitor and accuse him of discarding everything he once believed in. When people stand up to the authority they once supported, we tend to see them as abandoning their previous principles. Terms such as *traitor* and *hypocrite* are often brandished against them like weapons by people who once were their closest allies. How could Paul so easily check his values at the door? His sense of duty? His belief in the goodness of his country?

A closer look at Paul's story reveals that he may not have changed as much as it seems. "I still believe in this country, its tremendous history, its example, and its potential," he says. "America is in a constant state of beta. It's always getting better, and there are people who are always trying to improve it, especially in these challenging times."

Paul hadn't abandoned his worldview, at least not wholesale. He still believed in the basic principles on which he saw his country as being based—goodness, fairness, and duty—and felt strongly committed to that country. His rebellious behavior was not hypocritical or an abandonment of those principles; it was an attempt to integrate them with the realities he had witnessed in Iraq. Perhaps the United States still stood for those values, even though it hadn't quite fulfilled them yet.

According to psychologists, the technical term for what was happening to Paul's worldview is *accommodation*. Researchers Stephen Joseph of the University of Warwick and P. Alex Linley of the University of Leicester have studied in detail the process of making sense of traumatic experiences. According to Joseph and Linley, people have a natural desire to be consistent—or, as the researchers call it, a completion tendency. We're happy when our most cherished beliefs about the world actually line up with the way the world is. When things are otherwise, as often happens when trauma challenges our worldview, we feel a strong emotional pull to settle the conflict.

In his book *What Doesn't Kill Us*, Joseph offers an intriguing analogy. Imagine you own an expensive porcelain vase, one you dearly love, and one day you stumble and accidentally knock the vase to the floor, shattering it. What's your initial impulse? If you're like most people, you want to repair it. This means supergluing the vase together, attempting to make it look exactly as it did before. But no matter how hard you try, this often isn't feasible. Some pieces may be lost; others may be too small to glue. So, if you can't put everything back the way it was, the best you may be able to do is assemble the pieces in a new way that is functional and still beautiful.

Trauma shatters our assumptive worldview. After facing serious traumas such as combat, assault, natural disaster, or life-threatening illness, it's often impossible for people simply to push the Reset button and return to their previous rosy beliefs. Continuing to believe that the world is safe and that good things happen to good people requires victims to overlook the reality of the trauma, or at least fool themselves into thinking the trauma wasn't so bad. For many people, such a convenient solution isn't possible. So they have to do their best to accommodate what has happened.

Paul hadn't abandoned his country and he hadn't abandoned his beliefs. He was merely trying to piece them back together given what he had experienced. But life isn't always as easy to reassemble as porcelain.

———

Army specialist Casey Sheehan arrived in Iraq with the First Calvary Division out of Fort Hood in April of 2004, just weeks after Paul Rieckhoff left Baghdad. Casey was from a strong Catholic, blue-collar family. His parents couldn't afford to send him to college, and joining the army meant, among other things, a twenty-thousand-dollar signing bonus that would pay for school. His family wasn't happy about it, but they supported his decision. Besides, Casey's recruiter promised him a post off the frontlines as a chaplain's assistant, which would mean he'd never see combat. The recruiter broke his promise.

As Paul Rieckhoff took to the airwaves that month, Casey joined in a rescue mission in Iraq. En route, his convoy was ambushed. Casey got off a couple of shots before he was killed. He was twenty-four years old. CNN reported the daily casualties while the Sheehan family was eating Sunday dinner. They weren't sure, but they thought they heard Casey's name. A few hours later, three military officers arrived at the house and told Cindy Sheehan that her oldest son was dead. "After what seemed an eternity," she writes in her 2005 book, *Not Another Mother's Child*, "I finally began to wonder who or what was making those horrible screaming noises. Then I realized it was me." These are the sounds of someone's world crumbling to pieces.

Cindy Sheehan's story follows beats similar to Paul Rieckhoff's. Like Paul, Cindy had been raised to believe that her country was good and just, a patriotic sentiment she passed to Casey. Also like Paul, Cindy had questions for her government. She wrote letters to Secretary of Defense Donald Rumsfeld in which she asked why American children were fighting a war without the proper training, equipment, or armor. She wrote to White House spokesperson Dana Perino, urging the government to bring the troops home so that no other innocent people like Casey would be killed.

But Cindy's and Paul's stories diverge here. Like Paul Rieckhoff, Cindy Sheehan struggled to accommodate what had happened, to refashion her worldview into something like what it had been before her son's untimely death. Unlike Paul, however, Cindy found this impossible to accomplish.

When Paul's worldview was challenged, he was able to alter it to fit his new sense of reality without abandoning it completely. He still believed in the inherent goodness and fairness of his country, yes. But he also realized that things had gone awry. So he committed himself to trying to fix them. The terrain of his beliefs had changed, but the ground beneath his feet was still fundamentally firm. For Cindy, such smooth accommodation was impossible. Talk to her for just a few minutes and you get a sense of her desperate struggle even to find all the pieces of her shattered worldview. The shards of her once-comforting beliefs about herself, her family, and her country lay strewn, and she couldn't figure out how to reassemble them.

Some psychologists believe that the emotional upheaval, the nightmares, flashbacks, anxiety, guilt, and fear often experienced by people suffering from posttraumatic stress disorder are precisely the result of losing these stabilizing beliefs. Although Paul's worldview was able to accommodate his traumatic experience, there's no guarantee that accommodation will be successful for everyone. Just as there are many ways to reassemble porcelain shards, there are limitless ways to reconstruct one's worldview, some of which are probably more helpful than others.

One particularly difficult outcome of worldview reconstruction is known as overaccommodation. As University of Missouri psychologists Patricia Resick and Monica Schnicke write in the *Journal of Consulting and Clinical Psychology*, "without good social support, or guidance by a therapist, the accommodation may be maladaptive and extreme." It's all too easy to arrive at conclusions such as "The world is an awful place," "No one can be trusted," and, perhaps worst of all, "I'm a bad person." In research published in the journal *Psychological Trauma*, psychologists Heather Littleton and Amie Grills-Taquechel surveyed more than three hundred and fifty college women who had been sexually assaulted. A staggering 45 percent had overaccommodated. For them, the world was a scary place and they were no longer the good people they once thought they were.

———

Cindy Sheehan was raised in a fairly traditional household in Bellflower, California. Her father worked at Lockheed, at the time one of the largest U.S. defense contractors. As an adult, Cindy was a youth minister at St. Mary's Catholic Church and organized after-school programs for at-risk middle school children.

Prior to Casey's death, Cindy felt she was a good mother, a good wife, and a good person who lived in a good country with good intentions. But now, inexplicably, her oldest son was dead, and Cindy blamed herself and the naïve faith in her country that she had passed to her son. There was no justification for his death, just as there now seemed to be no rationalization for her worldview. In *Not Another Mother's Child*, Cindy wrote, "I was raised in a country by a public school system that taught us that America was good, that America was just. America has been killing people . . . since we first stepped on this continent; we have been responsible for death and destruction." Of her prior belief in a good and just America, she said, "I passed on that bullshit to my son and my son enlisted."

Cindy's assumptive worldview was shattered nearly beyond recognition after Casey's death. It was painfully clear to her now that the world was not the safe place she once believed it to be. "I don't trust anything anymore," she says from her home in Vacaville, California. If there is a theme to her story, that's it: loss of trust. "The army promised to take care of Casey, and now Casey was dead. The government was lying to everybody. The president misused his authority to exploit America's resources and kill American children. I grew up in the Vietnam era, and I was a history major. History is full of stories of governments lying to their people and exploiting them. I knew that when Casey enlisted. I never trusted our government, but I thought the government had our best interest in mind. So now, eight years after Casey's death, I know any form of trust of any institution was terrible and tragically misplaced. Now my eyes are fully opened."

Cindy is something of a living picket sign. She communicates with her body as much as with her voice, which is gently fierce and clear. She wears her intentions in the deep lines of her face, in a sympathetic look or a biting glare. Her strawberry blond hair is cut in a mother's short, utilitarian style, parted to one side. She would show up at rallies dressed down in T-shirts and jeans, always with a cogent message for policy makers.

"I wasn't thinking so much in terms of good or bad anymore, just in terms of wrong or right," she says. "For instance, I would have thought before Casey died that it was bad to go to jail." She smiles. "Now it's my duty." Cindy's been arrested at rallies, she estimates, fifteen or sixteen times.

Though she often caught the attention of the police, she was finding it harder to get her message out to the public. There was no unified antiwar pro-justice voice. By this time, eighteen hundred American troops had been killed. The president, who was spending a nearly five-week-long working vacation at his Texas ranch just outside Crawford, was now arguing to stay the course in Iraq to honor the sacrifices of the ones who had fallen. "I was so full of rage and feeling so helpless and like such a failure after all the work for peace that I had done," Cindy writes in her memoir. "Why would I want another person to go through what I'd gone through for this war?" One hot August day in 2005, Cindy had had enough.

President Bush's family ranch sits on fifteen hundred acres of brush-covered prairie buttressed by the Rainey Creek and the Middle Bosque River. Cattle graze on the land amid small rock outcroppings and groves of big oak. At its heart is the russet, flat limestone house where the president met with foreign leaders ranging from Russian president Vladimir Putin to British prime minister Tony Blair.

That August, on the side of the road, just beyond the ranch, Cindy Sheehan and forty others set up base camp, soon to be dubbed Camp Casey. Here she would stay, she announced, until she was granted a face-to-face meeting with the president. Cindy and a group of mothers had met with the president once before. Her grief was fresh then, and she didn't say much. This second meeting would be very different, though. She would demand of the president, "Every time you get out there and say that you're going to continue the killing in Iraq to honor the fallen heroes, you say, 'except Casey Sheehan' . . . You don't have my permission."

In the beginning, Camp Casey hosted about a hundred supporters a day. Counterprotesters shouting pro-Bush slogans sprouted up along the side of the road. In response, fifteen hundred people gathered at a park in Crawford for a peace demonstration. As support for Cindy's cause grew, Camp Casey installed a memorial display of a thousand white crosses, stars, and crescents, bearing the names of fallen soldiers in Iraq. According to Cindy, in mid-August, sixteen hundred antiwar candlelight vigils in support of her son were held around the country. The camp was visited by such celebrities as Martin Sheen, Reverend Al Sharpton, Joan Baez, and several members of Congress.

As the Camp Casey demonstration lingered on late into the month of August, Cindy appeared on nearly every major national news program with her simple message: end the war and bring our fighting sons and daughters home before it's too late.

The president finally responded to Cindy, but not face-to-face. Speaking to reporters, he said, "I strongly support her right to protest. There's a lot of people protesting. And there's a lot of points of view about the Iraq War. As you know, in Crawford last weekend, there was people from both sides of the issue or from all sides of the issue there to express their opinions . . . She expressed her opinion. I disagree with it. I think immediate withdrawal from Iraq would be a mistake. I think those who advocate immediate withdrawal from not only Iraq but the Middle East are advocating a policy that would weaken the United States. So I appreciate her right to protest. I understand her anguish. I've met with a lot of families. She doesn't represent the view of a lot of families I have met with."

After airing this clip of the president on MSNBC's program *Hardball*, host Chris Matthews welcomed his guest panel. "It seems to me what's happening now is not just this back-and-forth about will the president meet with Cindy Sheehan or not?" posed Matthews. "But both sides now seem to be saying, because there are casualties in this war, two thousand dead now . . . that's proof we should not fight anymore, we should pull out. And the other side says, well, we have had casualties—that's the president speaking—we should stay in, because we owe it to them." He then turned to his panel. "Paul Rieckhoff, your view? Do you think it's fair to use the dead . . . to make a case for a policy?"

"I honestly don't think so," Paul said in the studio at MSNBC. He had long since replaced his flak jacket with the sharp suit and tie he wore for national media interviews. "I think this all stems from the president's failure to articulate what success looks like. He has never communicated to the American public, to the Iraqi people, and to the troops on the ground what 'right' looks like."

Trauma challenged and changed Paul Rieckhoff's worldview. Though he asked himself a lot of hard questions, to this day he still believes in his country. Though he recognizes that mistakes have been made, he hasn't lost faith in America altogether. Though he sees clearly that the United States isn't completely good or just, he still has confidence that it aspires to goodness and justice. As the founder and executive director of Iraq and Afghanistan Veterans of America, he is at the helm of one of the largest nonpartisan advocacy groups in the country, with more than two hundred thousand members. He regularly appears on shows such as *Meet the Press*, *Anderson Cooper 360*, and *Real Time with Bill Maher*, sometimes defending and sometimes countering American policy decisions. Five years after he returned home from Iraq, *GQ* ranked him thirty-seven out of the fifty most powerful people in Washington, DC.

After adjusting his worldview, Paul also adjusted his role—from soldier to activist. However broad the divide between these two roles, Paul still viewed the world through the lens of social accountability. His accommodated worldview left him still serving his country and still seeing his life as making sense, unlike Cindy Sheehan, who found there was simply no way to understand the world as she had before her son's death.

The stark difference between their two paths is seen in the final moments of that August 23, 2005, interview on *Hardball*. "You agree, though, Paul, that pulling out now, yanking the plug, sending the troops home in the next couple of weeks and months, would be bad news?" asked Chris Matthews. Given Paul's story, it may seem surprising that he responded in the affirmative. America should not pull out of Iraq, Paul believed, as Cindy Sheehan was demanding. "I think it is unrealistic, and I also think it's morally irresponsible," he said. "I think, at this point, we do have an obligation to the Iraqi people."

"Most Americans assume they have to be with President Bush and 'Stay-the-Course,' or be with Cindy Sheehan and 'Bring 'em Home Right Now.' Neither mantra is realistic," Paul wrote in a 2006 *Huffington Post* article. A third choice, he argued, was calling on the most socially accountable people in the country. "Pull all the living former presidents into Washington. Get Secretaries Albright, Powell, Brzezinski, and Kissinger there. Add military experts ranging from General Schwarzkopf to General Batiste to General Zinni to General Clark. Get the best Middle East experts in America. And don't forget the Iraq Vets. The President and Congress must show some real leadership and get our country's best people, not just the agreeable ones, all working together to offer new plans and ideas." Paul believed that, much like his worldview, the solution didn't have to be one way or the other—the truth lay somewhere in the middle.

After Cindy's twenty-six-day vigil outside President Bush's Crawford ranch, he still refused to meet her. Instead, he ended his vacation early. Before Camp Casey rolled up its tents, Cindy announced the next phase of her protest. She called it the Bring Them Home Now Tour. It would follow the president to New Orleans after Hurricane Katrina obliterated the city, and then onto the sidewalks outside the White House. Cindy's demonstration covered forty-two cities in twenty-six states. It solidified her reputation as one of the most highly polarizing figures in America, both loved and reviled, sometimes by the same people, depending on what she posted online on a given day. She continues to be at the forefront of political activism, demonstrating everywhere from Martha's Vineyard to Oslo, Norway, to Sacramento, where she was arrested as part of the Occupy Wall Street movement.

From housewife to infamous revolutionary, she's spent her life since Casey's death working to shake others' worldviews. She has written a series of books and booklets, including one that challenges people's positive assumptions about America. Called *Myth America: 10 Greatest Myths of the Robber Class and the Case for Revolution,* it conveys her intense doubts about fundamental beliefs, ranging from "American has a free press" to "elections matter."

Two supersurvivors, two rebels. But trauma touched their lives in vastly different ways, leaving one of them still a firm believer in the basic goodness of his nation and the other a deep cynic. From both sides of this chasm, however, they have influenced their country in ways not soon to be forgotten. It's comforting to know that no matter where we fall in our thinking, we have the power to endure after surviving a catastrophic event. Even while one course is considerably harder to take than the other, this presents an interesting conundrum: in the end, regardless of whether one believes the world is a safe place, haven't we just replaced one perception, or delusion, for another?

———

"People aren't obstinate; their minds are," Dan Tapster says. He had just produced a *MythBusters* experiment to test whether it was possible for a child on a swing to complete a full three-hundred-and-sixty-degree arch. After trying and failing at more reasonable approaches, *MythBusters* concluded that it would be virtually impossible unless they attached powerful rockets to the swing. Despite the evidence, once again some viewers cried foul.

"Certain people refused to believe our conclusion because they said they had *actually done it* when they were kids!" says Dan. "They *believed* they had actually done it. You have to conclude that there are some false beliefs people hold on to that they believe to be fundamentally true."

Yes, it's unlikely that all these viewers were lying, though the prospect that they're delusional doesn't seem any more appealing. But then again, stories such as Paul's and Cindy's remind us that we're all a bit delusional, clinging to polite fictions until we can't anymore, because the alternative would be too difficult to bear. The producers of *MythBusters* are truly fighting an uphill battle.

5

The Company We Keep

I would rather walk with a friend in the dark
than alone in the light.
—HELEN KELLER

People rarely recover from accidents such as Amanda Wigal's.

On a morning in June 2007, Bartlett Lake was buzzing with jet skiers and wakeboard boats as Amanda's crew of urbane Sea Ray shipmates sunned on the deck. Music wafted through the air, ricocheting from hip-hop to country to rock.

The captain of the party boat, Amanda was in her mid-twenties, small and slim with dust-colored hair that framed high cheekbones and kind eyes. Her outgoing personality, in company with her openness and natural beauty, charmed nearly everyone she met. To know Amanda was to love her.

Amanda's fiancé, Jeremy, maneuvered the boat into a small cove and anchored it. Amanda brought out sandwiches, and someone opened the cooler. When the day got too hot, they all stripped down to their swimsuits and jumped into the water underneath a vast Arizona sky. Jeremy attached the inner tube to the back of the boat. It was big and yellow, with twin handles. Amanda swam out to the tube and pulled her slight physique inside it. She turned and faced the sky, resting her legs against the inner tube so that only her feet touched the water. She squinted into the sun and waved to Jeremy, who was standing at the wheel of the boat flashing a confident grin, his hand on the throttle. Amanda gripped the inner tube handles in anticipation. The speedboat propeller burbled the placid water to life. Then the boat took off, tugging Amanda's inner tube behind it. The flurry of wind and speed made Amanda feel invigorated and alive.

From the periphery, Amanda noticed a big white vessel cruising on the wrong side of the lake. Maritime rules controlled unmarked water lanes, dividing the lake like a multilane two-way highway. But not everyone knew the rules, and this misguided cruiser was coming toward them. Jeremy, who had a lot of experience on pontoons and speedboats, noticed the oncoming traffic, too. Thinking quickly, he veered the speedboat away, but he miscalculated, turning a fraction of a moment too late. The speedboat arched away from the cruiser, but Amanda's inertia swung her into the oncoming vessel. Her head slammed against the hull so hard that the blow knocked her unconscious and sent dark blood cascading into the lake.

A helicopter airlifted her to Scottsdale Healthcare Osborn Medical Center, where she was listed in critical condition. Comatose, she was later moved to St. Joseph's Hospital and Medical Center. During her first critical days in intensive care, nurses noted that a seemingly endless pageant of people filed in and out of Amanda's room. Friends from every part of her life came to see her as she fought for her life. They stayed by her side every day, held her hands, and told her how much she meant to them. "We love you," they said. "You can make it!"

Jeremy wasn't so sure. The neurologists said that Amanda was brain dead and would not recover. The accident replayed in his head with pristine clarity as he searched for any way out of what had happened. But every version of the story ended with Jeremy pulling his fiancée from the water with blood rushing out of the gash in her head. In the pale light of her hospital room, his bride-to-be looked as though she were sleeping. Though she had been beautiful, the accident and the weeks-long coma had altered her loveliness. Her skin was as white as the hospital gown that covered her. Her face was buried in heavy bandages. She was intubated, and her breathing was thin and even.

For Amanda's friends and family, it must have been hard to reconcile this version of her with the vivacious person they knew—the free-spirited college sorority girl, the spontaneous postgrad who was all in for flirty poolside weekends and sprees to the slopes of Utah and the shores of Puerto Vallarta. Amanda was the first person to admit she wasn't goal-directed. She was young, and she had her whole life ahead of her. She lived in her grandparents' old condo, which was fully paid for, so discretionary income funded getaways and nights on the town, where she drank with her friends, frequented clubs, and danced. Her friends had nicknamed her Chatty Cathy because all the guys talked to her. Now Amanda might not ever talk again.

Weeks with little change in her condition forced her family and friends to reach an impossible conclusion: Amanda was lost. Neurosurgeons informed them that keeping Amanda alive was only postponing the inevitable. Previously encouraging, upbeat visits turned into opportunities to say good-bye.

At which point, Amanda woke up.

———

Doctors tend to call cases like Amanda's miraculous because of their extremely infrequent occurrence. It's not every day that people with injuries as serious as Amanda's open their eyes again. But we want to avoid painting a picture of supersurvivors as supermen of sorts, who can overcome even death. Amanda certainly doesn't regard herself this way. As we will see, she exemplifies many of the inner resources we celebrate in other chapters, such as grounded hope and a strong sense of personal control. But she doesn't credit these characteristics with her eventual supersurvivorship. Indeed, given her comatose state, marshaling inner resources may not be what brought her back from the brink. For that we should look outside of her, to the love and care she received from others.

"Amanda was always outgoing and had more friends than she knew what to do with," says Iris Wigal, Amanda's mother. "She was never one to sit at home. She liked being a part of something, liked being involved."

And perhaps this is precisely what made the difference. Amanda would later speculate that, even through the opaque fog of her comatose state, she was somehow aware of the presence of her loved ones in the room with her. Although medical science can't say for sure, Amanda might not have survived without the support of all these people. "I couldn't believe how many people came to visit," says Amanda. "My friends, my mom's friends, people who grew up with me, people I hadn't seen in a long time. Without them, who do you have to recover for?"

According to dozens of studies, the people in our lives really matter. Psychologists Kathryn Herbst-Damm and James Kulik, for instance, wanted to find out if social support really could make a difference in cases where life and death were at stake. In a 2005 study published in the journal *Health Psychology*, they followed two hundred and ninety patients from the moment they were admitted to hospice care to the time they died. These were very sick people; hospice is normally offered only to those with no more than six months to live. Most hospice organizations couldn't function without a core group of volunteers available to visit patients to provide emotional and practical support. About a third of the patients in this study specifically requested and received visits from just such volunteers, while the remaining two-thirds didn't.

The care and dedication that hospice volunteers display as they accompany people in the final stage of life make them nothing short of angels. But they're not angels of the supernatural sort, and they don't possess superhuman healing powers. That's what makes the results of this study all the more intriguing: The rate at which the patients who were visited by volunteers passed away was almost a third that of those who were not visited. The lives of the former lasted more than two and a half months longer, an eternity to someone hoping to live long enough to witness the birth of a grandchild or to celebrate one last Christmas.

This isn't an isolated finding. In a much larger study, published in 1997 in the *American Journal of Epidemiology*, a group of researchers headed by Brenda Penninx followed nearly three thousand people for almost two and a half years, investigating the connection between social support and mortality as part of the ambitious Longitudinal Aging Study Amsterdam. The random sample was drawn from municipalities all over the Netherlands, was stratified by age and sex, and included ordinary adults, living at home, who ranged in age from fifty-five to eighty-five. In short, it was the kind of high-quality study you'd do if you wanted firm answers to big questions.

The researchers assessed the amount of social support in people's lives in a number of ways, including whether they were married or had a partner, their total number of friends and family, and the participants' personal assessments of the quality of support received. But the most important factor appeared to be the emotional support itself. Twenty-nine months later, they accessed public records to track mortality, expecting some portion of the participants to have died naturally from conditions ranging from heart disease or cancer to accident or simply old age. They found that those study participants who received moderate to high levels of emotional support were about half as likely to have died than those who received lower levels of support. About 13 percent of people with low emotional support had died, compared to only about 6 percent of people with moderate to high emotional support. So, social support may help people literally survive—an important prerequisite for being a supersurvivor of course.

On the psychological front, many studies have shown that aspects of social support appear to provide a buffer to the emotional effects of trauma and other negative circumstances, helping to protect some people from mental health symptoms that haunt others. It's also one of the predictors of posttraumatic growth, the tendency of some individuals to find benefits in the aftermath of tragedy.

We've already met supersurvivors who have acquired, and relied upon, the support of many. Asha Mevlana, in her post-cancer journey to become an internationally renowned musician, has amassed thousands of supportive fans all over the world, who have in turn bolstered her emotionally. Paul Rieckhoff couldn't have gained the support he needed to start the Iraq and Afghanistan Veterans of America organization without the national exposure that enabled him to rally hundreds of thousands of veterans and followers to action. Even Alan Lock, who traversed, blind, the second-largest body of water in a rowboat, did so with the love and support of friends and family, who gave him the strength and encouragement to succeed.

None of these people claimed they became supersurvivors on their own.

But isn't there a dark side to relying on others? Relationships can be less than perfect. Sometimes people disappoint us, distance themselves, or turn their backs. At first Amanda Wigal's story seems simple, but like all aspects of posttrauma recovery, there's so much more just under the surface.

———

Amanda's visitors liked to bring her gifts, flowers, get-well cards, magazines, and books. When she opened a magazine, words swam on the page. The meaning of the letters, somehow familiar, was missing. Amanda's memory was foggy. The flotsam of names, faces, and places floated in her mind, unanchored to meaning or context.

Visiting hours at the hospital began early. Each day, people with familiar faces, recognized from some murky place and time, appeared in her room. They spoke to her. Sometimes she replied. Words spilled from her mouth in a gush of broken sounds. Her responses elicited confusion. Her brain was a broken machine, its wires frayed, its mechanisms unhinged.

Today, what Amanda does remember of her time in the hospital comes to her in cockeyed scenes. "I asked a nurse to dial my mother's phone number," says Amanda. "When she answered, I told her I was stranded on the side of I-17 and she had to come pick me up. I packed everything and waited for her to come get me."

And some of these memories, says Amanda, weren't memories at all but the effects of medication generating dreams that spilled into her reality, dreams such as one of the hospital staff killing patients and putting the bodies into beds.

Then there was the morning Amanda woke up in the wrong bed, in the wrong room, in the wrong building. The right half of her body was still weak when she stumbled out of bed, balancing herself against the rail. Tiptoeing past the nurses' station, she edged along the wall without stumbling once. At an elevator bank, she pushed the Down button. She'd leave the floor and find a phone. But whom would she call? *My mom*, she thought. *I'll call my mom and tell her where I am.* But where was she? It didn't matter; her mom would find her, would straighten things out, would set things right. As the door opened, a hand touched her shoulder. Amanda turned and said something. It came out in French, a language she had studied in college. This was how Amanda learned she was in a secure unit at Barrow Neurological Institute, and that she wasn't going anywhere. She attempted a half dozen other escapes, but never got far. Security attached a bracelet to her ankle that sounded an alarm if she left the floor. When that didn't stop her, they strapped her to beds and wheelchairs.

Amanda's increasing cognitive abilities were a mixed blessing— good enough to attempt escapes but not good enough to realize that escape wasn't necessary. The friends who had once poured into her room to wish her good-bye now had no idea how to help her. What could they say? What could they do? It was strange. When she was presumed dead, it was easy for friends to support her. Now that she was alive, friends were barely around.

"I watched Amanda's social support drop off completely," says her mother. "It was hard on Amanda after the accident because the dynamics of her relationships changed. To all of a sudden lose them—it hurt her deeply. I wanted to convince people that she wasn't going to be any different now than the girl she was." But the around-the-clock care she required, and the years of intense rehabilitation ahead of her, meant that Amanda was different now.

Even her fiancé, Jeremy, faced uncertainty about how to connect with her. A few weeks earlier, at a surprise party at the Fox Sports Grill, where they'd first met, he had fallen to one knee and proposed to her in front of all their friends. Now he was faced with the possibility of, at best, taking care of a severely disabled woman for the rest of her life. He found himself in the most difficult situation of his life, and he wouldn't have been human if he hadn't considered turning around and leaving.

Amanda isn't alone in her experience of diminishing social support. Decades of research have documented a complex dance between sufferers and helpers following tragedy. The first step goes something like this: Shortly after a disaster, people line up to offer support in a great outpouring of empathy and assistance. This can be seen clearly in almost every natural disaster of the last century. In the aftermath of the 2010 earthquake that killed more than two hundred thousand people in Haiti and displaced more than a million others, people and organizations around the globe reacted generously and heroically. Governments pledged more than five billion dollars in aid, and humanitarian workers poured into the beleaguered country.

Psychologists Krzysztof Kaniasty of Georgia State University and Fran Norris of Indiana University of Pennsylvania have spent more than two decades exploring how the help that people offer in the aftermath of tragedies impacts victims. Writing in the journal *Current Directions in Psychological Science*, they have called this the "heroic phase" of disaster support, and it seems to happen following virtually every collective tragedy.

But organizations and individuals simply don't have the energy or resources to keep up such heroics forever. After a time, people cut back on the amount of assistance they give, whether it's monetary, practical, or emotional. When the need is great, this can leave important jobs undone. According to CBS News, six months after the Haitian earthquake, 98 percent of the rubble remained uncleared. With little transitional housing built, the number of people living in tents and makeshift shelters in relief camps had risen to a shocking 1.6 million. Even a year later, a report published by Oxfam noted, "Despite the success of emergency lifesaving aid after last year's earthquake, long-term recovery from the disaster has barely begun." And, infamously, the cholera outbreak that was likely inadvertently carried to Haiti by UN peacekeepers in October of 2010 remains difficult to stem, despite continued efforts years later.

The reality is that victims received a lot of support in the immediate aftermath of the earthquake. Billions of dollars were disbursed. Thousands of good people traveled to Haiti to lend a hand, some of whom remained there for years. As the Oxfam report mentioned, this support saved countless lives in the immediate aftermath of the quake. There certainly were problems: help was sometimes slow to arrive, was misdirected, or was not offered in the ways needed. But almost no amount of support could keep pace with the level of need the Haitian people were experiencing, a disheartening and frustrating reality for victims and aid workers alike. One aid worker, Quinn Zimmerman, expressed these feelings on NPR's *Talk of the Nation*. Commenting on the source of his frustration, he said, "I think the combination for me was the realization that no matter how much I tried to help here, or I've tried to help here, and continue to try to help here, there's no way that I can fix this place."

This drawing down of social support isn't unique to Haiti. It's a predictable stage in most disaster-relief scenarios, according to Norris and Kaniasty. "The initial period of intense affiliation, heroic sacrifice, and altruism eventually gives rise to the harsh reality of grief, loss, and destruction," they wrote in the *Journal of Personality and Social Psychology* in 1996, years before the Haitian quake. Good Samaritans are only human. Despite the best of intentions, there is only so much they are capable of doing, and there is only so much emotional energy available to invest. It's hard to be heroic all the time.

So, despite the enormous level of support they've actually received, survivors can be left with the perception that nobody cares. These two predictable stages of social support led Kaniasty and Norris, among others, to question the findings showing that social support was psychologically helpful. They wondered if earlier research had conflated *received* social support with *perceptions* that social support would be available in the future, if needed. Disaster victims may perceive that future support will not be available, even though they have already received enormous amounts of support. If these two aspects of social support could be teased apart, the researchers wondered, which one would really be helpful for victims?

To help answer this question, Norris and Kaniasty interviewed 498 adult survivors of Hurricane Hugo six months after the category-four storm devastated large areas of North and South Carolina in 1989, killing 33 and forcing tens of thousands of people into temporary shelters. The U.S. Federal Emergency Management Agency, or FEMA, was famously criticized for its slow response to this disaster. Nonetheless, helpers from across the country showed up en masse to lend a hand. The Red Cross and the Salvation Army both offered funds and aid workers to assist victims of the storm. Two hundred million dollars in federal aid and other disaster-response measures, such as temporary housing assistance, were mobilized in the region.

Six months after the disaster, in addition to asking questions about the degree to which victims' lives were concretely impacted by the trauma through losses and injuries, the researchers asked the victims about the kinds of support they had actually received from others, and their perceptions that such support would be available in the future should they need it. The results seem discouraging: the more severe the victims' losses and injuries, the less support they perceived would be available to them in the future. Kaniasty and Norris have dubbed this the perceived social support deterioration effect. Strangely, aid organizations say that the situation is just the opposite: their policy is to offer the people with the greatest need more help than those who haven't been as severely impacted. But that's not what the victims perceived.

Some of Kaniasty and Norris's additional findings may shed light on this alarming disconnect. They found that the actual level of support received by victims in the aftermath of the disaster didn't seem related to those victims' emotional well-being. Instead, the victims' subjective perception that support was available strongly predicted their emotional well-being. So, even if people actually once received a lot of support, they might perceive that it is not now available or that it would not be in the future, and this perception is what really seems to matter in terms of victims' emotions.

These results point to an intriguing truth that cuts across many areas of psychological research: reality and perception are two separate things, and they're not always as related as you'd think. It's not that they're not related at all. It's just that, in this case, the relationship isn't very strong. Depending on how these two things are measured in different studies, the relationship ranges from moderate to virtually nonexistent.

As we've mentioned, Good Samaritans' efforts tend to fade with time. So even though victims have actually gotten a lot of support, they're sometimes left with the very realistic perception that it won't be available in the long term. Other times, support is in fact still available even though people might not perceive that it is. Science can't yet provide a firm explanation for why this disconnect between reality and perception occurs. But one of the most intriguing hypotheses is a kind of contrast effect: no matter how much actual support is offered, it's often outstripped by the amount of support needed. This certainly was the case in Haiti. So even if support is continuously available, the gap between what aid workers are capable of doing and the amount of need that is still present seems huge, leaving victims to perceive that real help simply isn't available.

To be clear, we aren't saying that people's heroic support efforts in the aftermath of tragedy are useless. These efforts often literally save people's lives by providing needed medical care, food, shelter, and services. We're also not saying that victims are ungrateful for the help they receive or are overly needy, or that aid organizations shouldn't try harder to meet victims' needs. The victims are in legitimate need because they've suffered unthinkable events. But this legitimate need can be so large that no supportive efforts could ever fully meet it. This isn't the victims' fault; it's the result of a set of horrific circumstances. The concrete support efforts offered in the aftermath of tragedy, however, don't seem as effective as one might expect at buffering victims from the *emotional* impact of the trauma. Instead, what seems more effective in this regard is victims' perception that support will continue to be accessible when it is needed.

So survivors often face a double challenge. First, they must confront the stress associated with living through a horrific event. But second, and perhaps equally as difficult to stomach, they must face the perceptions of estrangement and isolation that so often slowly creep up afterward.

Amanda encountered many of the same obstacles that disaster victims face: her friends distanced themselves after their initial outpouring of support; her needs seemed just too great for them to bear. Despite this situation, it may seem odd that Amanda never felt the sense of estrangement we've been discussing. When you ask her how she survived, how she bounced forward and ended up becoming more than she thought she ever could be before the accident, she claims it was due to unwavering social support. She remained confident that social support would always be available. Of all of the many disconnects that now made up Amanda's world, this divide was the widest and the most perplexing to bridge.

———

Though it seemed innocuous to her at the moment, the mishap with the desk drawer would confront Jane McGonigal with many of the same challenges that Amanda faced.

For the past decade, McGonigal had immersed herself in researching virtual game play. A doctoral student at the University of California, Berkeley, her focus was on the real skills and abilities that gamers were building that could transfer to real-life contexts and real-world problem solving.

McGonigal, a brilliant researcher and game designer who doesn't look or act like the stereotype of a Silicon Valley tech geek, manages to project intellectual sophistication without stuffy pretense. She wears a lot of sparkles, glitter, flashy boots, lightning bolt earrings, and other superhero jewelry. Combining the looks of a pixie with the mind of Einstein, she's disarmingly direct, quietly thoughtful, and deeply curious about people.

Her doctoral studies concerned the cross section of computer science and psychology. The work required her to spend a lot of time in her own head, which was fine because, despite her spunky appearance, she's a natural introvert. "I don't hang out with people very long before reaching my limit," she admits from underneath ringlets of blond hair. "I wouldn't normally answer my phone for friends. I've always lived in my own head. I could be jogging and pass my own mother without registering her." This isn't hyperbole. Jane often jogged through the streets of her home in San Francisco, removed from people and distractions, her thoughts singularly focused.

She jogged so much that her leg muscles became more powerful than she realized. So one day, when she bent down to refill her printer's paper tray, she stood up fast, and with full explosive force catapulted her head into an open cabinet. The impact propelled her brain against the top of her skull. An hour later, she was laid out, nauseated, dizzy, and disoriented. She'd given herself a concussion, usually a mild and temporary brain injury. The doctors told her the symptoms would last for up to three weeks. Until then, she would need to take it easy and give her brain the chance to heal.

But it didn't heal. A month passed, and she was not getting any better. "I knew something was wrong," she remembers. "I could read and write and speak, but my thinking felt compressed, and pretty soon my head would hurt to the point that I'd start to black out. I couldn't think about complex things anymore, and I'm a cerebral person."

Normally a happy and upbeat woman, McGonigal was now met with crippling depression. She had always been a super-high-achieving person. In the first half of 2009, at age thirty-one, she had launched two games and was writing a book. Productivity was crucial to her, and her mind was accustomed to working fast. After the accident, her functioning plummeted.

McGonigal found herself experiencing unexpected feelings of isolation. She looked completely normal from the outside, so friends treated her the same as always. Nobody seemed to get what was happening inside her skull. For the first time, aloneness didn't feel good to her because it meant she couldn't find the support she needed. She wondered if anyone could understand what she was going through, if anyone would ever truly be there for her in her growing fear and uncertainty.

Even more frightening, she was beginning to experience suicidal thoughts. The top of her building, forty-three stories above the city, offered a spectacular view, but McGonigal stopped going to the roof because she was afraid she would jump. It was day thirty-four since her concussion when she realized she had to do something about her suffering.

She needed people to bring her out of her head. The problem was she had groomed all her friends to be hands-off. "I needed people to connect with me in a different way," she says. "When someone's had a trauma, people don't know what to do or how to act." For instance, friends brought her bottles of wine, but she wasn't allowed to drink. They'd take her out of the apartment for coffee, but she wasn't supposed to have caffeine. She couldn't leave the apartment anyway without getting nauseated and feeling as though she would black out. It wasn't their fault. Most people wouldn't know what to do for someone in this situation. "I'd have to retrain them to be what I needed," she says.

In response to her pain, McGonigal began drafting the concept for a video game she called SuperBetter. It worked on a now-familiar premise. The science demonstrates that positive changes can occur in our lives as a direct result of our facing an extreme challenge, she explains. "Instead of being weakened by our obstacles, we could grow stronger." McGonigal believed that, with the right tools, people could use these obstacles as a springboard to unleash their best qualities and lead happier lives.

Players are trauma survivors. After signing in, the game prompts them to choose from a series of real-world quests designed to build what McGonigal calls social resilience. The quests are purposely easy and achievable, such as shaking someone's hand for a couple of seconds or sending someone a quick text message. SuperBetter encourages players to invite real-world allies (friends and family members) to the game, and these allies in turn send the players on more reality-based quests. For every successful quest, SuperBetter rewards players by increasing their resilience score, which measures physical, social, mental, and emotional resilience. The game also provides a forum for players to reach out and make new virtual allies—other players across the globe fighting the same foes, such as posttraumatic stress disorder, chronic illness, and severe abuse.

McGonigal had come to much the same conclusions that Kaniasty and Norris did in their research. Examining life after her head injury, she noted her tendency to feel alone, even when she had the full support of her husband and friends. On a personal level, she was noticing the social support deterioration effect, and it was impacting her well-being in profound ways. She yearned for a community of supportive people—people who really understood what she was going through and who would be there for her through thick and thin. For this, she would need to help her friends and family feel more comfortable with what she was going through and provide them with a concrete way to help her.

When SuperBetter first came online, it was slow to develop. But as people populated its virtual community, they began to connect and care for one another in real life. A player with acute myeloid leukemia used the game to maximize his quality of life through quests that made sure he got up, got dressed, and left his apartment every day to make one new memory. After playing the game for several weeks, a computer programmer in San Francisco revealed to a few friends and family members that he was suffering from depression and invited them to be allies, making him feel closer to and better understood by them.

McGonigal, too, was a SuperBetter player. "I had a notebook, and my husband kept a rudimentary scoring system and a list I wanted my day to include: creativity, showering, eating. I'd get three points for walking around the block. I called people to give them a concrete thing to do. It was better than saying, 'I'm messed up and I need your support.' Most people wouldn't know what to do in that situation. 'Just call me at night, for five minutes and ask how I'm doing.' My sister would say, 'Sit by window and see what you see.'"

With dozens of such interactions and tasks, even as small as many of them were, she began to realize that she in fact was not alone. Through the game, she began to perceive that support was available when she needed it.

Her experiences again echo Kaniasty and Norris's observations. In *Current Directions in Psychological Science*, they write that "beliefs of being reliably connected to other people will shield victims from experiencing intense distress." McGonigal discovered that a virtual sea of support was available for her to dip into, even though she previously perceived that she was in the midst of a desert. She found a way to prove to herself that people were there for her and would reliably continue to be.

There are important differences between Kaniasty and Norris's work and McGonigal's efforts. Kaniasty and Norris study large-scale communal disasters, whereas McGonigal is primarily concerned with how individuals cope with personal traumas. Also, Kaniasty and Norris simply observe how victims perceive the availability of social support in the aftermath of tragedy; McGonigal was trying to change those perceptions. Either way, it appears that the divide between reality and perception can be bridged.

———

Amanda and her mother, Iris, had always been close, but their relationship took on an even deeper meaning following the death of Amanda's father when she was twenty. After that, Amanda and her mother promised to be there for each other, however unimaginable the situation.

For thirty-three years Iris had been an elementary school teacher, but now she was retired. After Amanda's accident, instead of teaching ten- and eleven-year-olds, she worked with Amanda, who often seemed like a toddler herself. Iris placed flashcards with basic mathematical problems in front of her daughter. "Can you add these numbers?"

Jeremy helped in the effort, too. One afternoon, while he was doing the laundry, he noticed Amanda curled up on the sofa, contemplative, her body dappled in sunlight. "Hey there," he said, sitting down next to her. She registered a tiny smile. He handed her a shirt. She folded it, and then another, stacking them in neat piles. "One, two, three . . ." Jeremy said, counting the shirts out loud with her. She counted along. Though Jeremy didn't know it, he was taking a page from Jane McGonigal's playbook. Sometimes, at dinner, he quizzed Amanda on the color of the foods on her plate. In the car on the way to rehab, he drilled her on words that started with certain letters.

Even though Iris and Jeremy were patiently encouraging, Amanda knew how disabled she was, how long it took her to come up with each number and each word. She ached to get back to being the same bright, fun-loving woman she was before the accident. But every mental and physical struggle convinced her that this might not be possible, at least not completely.

Amanda moved in with her mother because she couldn't be left alone to take care of herself. "Recovery took about a year," Iris remembers. "I monitored everything. We made schedules for her day: get up, get dressed, brush your teeth. She had homework from the rehab clinic—detailed homework. She'd have questions for me. I'd double-check her answers and sit with her when she worked. Her math skills were gone. I mean, this was the girl who skipped two math levels in the third grade!"

Amanda had sustained an injury to part of her frontal lobes. Among the things she initially lost were specific memories of her life before the accident. She didn't remember, for instance, that she had been a sales manager at a small promotional products company. She didn't remember that the job was less than professionally satisfying, or that she had decided to jump ship but changed her mind when the owner announced he was retiring and offered to sell her the company. So after regaining her ability to communicate, Amanda unexpectedly learned that she was the owner of a small Scottsdale business called Brandables.

Partly to assume Amanda's loans and partly to provide her with a tangible goal for which to strive, Iris had taken over the day-to-day management of the company. "There was a sense that, as long as the company was waiting for Amanda, she would work hard to get back," Iris says.

Before the injury, Amanda's identity was not tied to the company to the extent that the latter might be used as a carrot for her recovery—not by a long shot. Iris was right, though. After the injury, getting back to Brandables was vital for Amanda. The company now represented a tangible goal to inspire her physical and cognitive recovery. Sometime between the boating accident and learning to function on the most basic human level, Brandables had become something more than just a job. It had become Amanda's lifeline.

"I knew people with my injury can't go back to their old lives," Amanda admits. "We have to make considerable adjustments." But she'd wanted badly to get back to a place where she could at least be independent and run Brandables, and she worked every day to get to that point. "The doctors said her recovery was astonishing," her mother remembers with a smile. "To see where she'd come from to where she was now. She was airlifted in; they said she was brain-dead. They told me to take her off the machines. She was ninety percent back to fully functioning. She got back to the company. It was a proud moment."

But it turned out to be far from ideal. In July of 2007, when Amanda slipped into a coma, the U.S. Commerce Department was showing economic growth, low unemployment, and rising wages across the country. Amanda returned to consciousness to find a new world paradigm. In the weeks she'd been comatose, the global economy had gone dark. Over the months, while she was regaining what she'd lost in the blink of an eye, stock and real estate prices plummeted. By December, Amanda was learning to speak again, and the labor markets were shedding hundreds of thousands of jobs.

Only three U.S. markets had lost more jobs than Greater Phoenix. High-end vendors folded, top restaurants shuttered their doors, and the area's trendiest spots failed. Shopping centers, at capacity two years ago, were down to a fraction of their occupancy. Of the fifteen suites in the complex where Brandables was situated, only five were now occupied. Like many companies, Brandables was suffering, too. So now Amanda was facing not only cognitive deficits, but also seemingly insurmountable economic deficits.

"I wanted Brandables to work. I needed it to, in fact," Amanda recalls with a note of tension. "I didn't give up on my rehab. How could I give up on my company?"

First, she did the painful math. The company simply didn't have the funds to continue paying its employees. As excruciating as it was, to make Brandables work, she would need to lay them off. In solidarity with this difficult decision, she stopped paying herself altogether. "I wasn't going to let the business go down without a fight. I couldn't keep the lights on, conduct business as usual, and still make a profit," she says. It was at this moment she realized that if she was going to stay in business and rebuild the company from the ground up, she was going to have to stop paying her mother, too.

Amanda found herself surrounded by lifeless racks of apparel and promotional samples in a silent two-thousand-square-foot office. She walked to the desk where her mom once sat, Iris's candy dish still on display. She passed empty cubicles and wandered through a short walkway into her warehouse, wondering how she was going to fulfill orders on her own.

Her memory was still weak, so she had to organize herself in such a way that clients' orders were always visible, otherwise she would forget about them. Sticky notes papered the walls. Whiteboards hanging in the hallways told Amanda about orders she had currently in process—those waiting for screen printing, embroidery, invoicing, or shipping. She operated the packing stations, hauled herself to trade shows, and became a member of the local chamber of commerce. But keeping up this pace on her own exhausted her and began doing her more harm than good.

"I couldn't let her fail," Iris says. "She's my daughter, and she will always be my daughter." So one morning, Iris quietly took up duties behind the sales counter. She would never ask for a paycheck. "I never claimed to have Amanda's business sense, but I had common sense. I didn't want to lose our bond."

Although Amanda had lost the support of friends and now walked the nearly vacant halls of a once-thriving business, she never once felt abandoned. "The funny thing was," she says with a reflective chuckle, "I never once sensed I was alone." To understand this, it's necessary to reflect on the distinction between actual social support and perceived support. Earlier we noted that it's possible to perceive that social support isn't available despite having received a lot of it. It's also possible to experience the opposite; Amanda perceived that she was immersed in a sea of support, even though most people objectively would say she was walking through a virtual desert. Perhaps this perception was due to the reliable efforts of Iris and Jeremy. No matter how many people peeled away from Amanda's life, she believed that her mother and fiancé would always be there for her. This bolstered her perception that support would be available for as long as she needed it, a belief which kept her going.

———

While more than two hundred thousand small businesses in the United States disappeared during the Great Recession, Amanda was able make Brandables one of the top twenty-five promotional distributors in Arizona. Even without the almost-fatal head trauma, this feat baffles the mind.

But what makes Amanda's story remarkable—indeed a story of supersurvivorship—isn't the million or so dollars the company has earned since its near bankruptcy. It is what happened within Amanda during both her physical and financial ordeals. Indeed, not all super-survivors are people who have changed the world. Supersurvival is often much more personal than that. Some people revolutionize their personal lives by seeing the world in new, more meaningful ways. Brandables started out being one thing and became something so much more to Amanda. "I *needed* to keep my company. Brandables suddenly meant everything to me. It became my identity. It went from being my livelihood to being my life," she says. Brandables carried on, even as store after store around it closed. Customers continued to come. Amanda and her mother filled orders. Today, Brandables is still run by mother and daughter.

To spend time with Amanda, one would hardly notice the scar above her forehead or the pauses she takes when she is pulling words from her mind. But she is different now, even if the changes aren't obvious. Since the accident and the loss of many of her former friends, Amanda has needed to rethink the party girl she once was. She spends more time alone. She isn't as social, and now enjoys being by herself much more than in large crowds. She calls this her newfound sense of quiet.

As soon as Amanda was able, and Jeremy felt he could take care of her, the two moved back in together. Their relationship had faced considerable adversity since Amanda's injury only weeks after Jeremy proposed marriage. But they had gotten through it. Despite uncertainties and challenges, Jeremy, like Iris, had remained by Amanda's side. Thirty-five months after the accident on Bartlett Lake, Jeremy and Amanda were married.

Amanda had discovered that, regardless of how many people surrounded her, two people would always be there for her. And believing that someone is by your side—someone who makes you smile, but also someone you know you can count on when you need support—is one of the great secrets to supersurvival.

6

Awakened by Death

Death destroys a man: the idea of Death saves him.
—E. M. FORSTER

Paul Watkins was a man on a mission. Having called the meeting with his business partners, he arrived at the office dressed in a shirt and tie, his dark hair neatly combed to the side, apprehension concealed behind the strength of newfound conviction. "Gentlemen," he started, placing his briefcase on the conference table, "it's been a great pleasure working with you, but I've decided to leave the company."

Mouths agape, his business partners sat stunned and silent. What was going to happen to the company? Over the years, Paul had grown it into a regional powerhouse. His plan had been to lead it to the next level, beyond Louisiana to the national market. He was the majority shareholder. All told, he was worth millions. What about his shares?

"I want you to buy me out for a song," he said to his bewildered investors. He'd promised them a great return, but selling his shares to them for a fraction of their value was utterly insane. Paul would be throwing away millions.

At his high-end apartment in New Orleans' prestigious St. Charles Avenue neighborhood, Paul opened his kitchen cabinets and removed dish after dish. Dinner plates, saucers, soup bowls, and coffee mugs clanked into trash bags. Standing at his closet, he gazed over the pressed collars and neat hems of the garments he'd worn to business deals all over the country. He yanked shirts and pants off hangers and bagged them to be given away. He donated the Oriental area rugs, the wall art, his television, and many of his books. It had to go. All of it.

Budgeting a weekly allowance of seventy-five dollars, he left his spacious apartment and moved into a twelve-by-fourteen-foot dirty beige room, swapping his grand window vista for a view of a school parking lot partially blocked by a rickety AC unit.

But he felt calmer and more surefooted than ever. Assuming he wasn't losing his mind, why would a sane man do this? "Yeah, I gave it up," Paul says with a jovial laugh. "I just sort of realized life is short." But Paul Watkins wasn't dying, at least no more than any other healthy man in his early forties. Nonetheless, he says, "I wanted to end my life differently."

***

Death is one of our society's last great taboos. If you doubt this, try bringing up the topic at the next dinner party. If you think talking about religion or money is socially inappropriate, just wait for the baffled looks you'll inspire when you start chatting about funeral homes and tombstones.

Most people avoid the topic—and not just in superficial ways. "About 80 percent of us will be physically dependent on others during the last months, weeks, or days of life," writes celebrated palliative care physician Ira Byock in his foreword to *The End-of-Life Handbook*. "We will need help with basic daily activities, including the biological needs of eating, personal hygiene, and elimination." For this reason, doctors almost unanimously agree that all adults should draw up a living will specifying what kind of medical care they would want if they were incapacitated and potentially nearing death. According to U.S. federal law, hospitals are obligated to ask patients if they have such documentation, presumably as a way of prompting them to consider it. Despite these facts, according to a 2008 report by the U.S. Department of Health and Human Services, only between 18 and 36 percent of people historically have a living will. The twenty minutes it takes to fill one out could mean the difference between life and death, but people generally decline to do so.

It's curious that we don't talk or even think about death more. After all, it's all around us—not in a gruesome or violent way usually, but as an inescapable fact of life. Think about it: There are seven billion people alive today; this means that there will be at least seven billion deaths within the next one hundred years. That's about seventy million deaths per year!

But perhaps the ubiquity and inevitability of death are exactly the reasons we don't think about the topic. Psychologists Sheldon Solomon, Tom Pyszczynski, and Jeff Greenberg have spent almost three decades investigating why and how people avoid thinking about death. These researchers' complex but very interesting conclusions are captured in a set of principles known collectively as terror management theory. They start with a simple observation: We human beings are the only animals able to step back and consider ourselves, our lives, and our futures. We ask pesky questions such as "Who am I?" "What should I be doing?" and "What does life have in store for me?" As a by-product of this self-reflective tendency, we can't help realizing that, ultimately, the future holds an end to our lives. We are mortal, and we know it. If we were logical creatures, *this would terrify us*. It's an inescapable death sentence that will be executed in only a few decades, and that's if we're not one of the unlucky ones struck down sooner by a fatal disease or an accident. But obviously most people aren't walking around in terror. Why not?

According to Solomon, Pyszczynski, and Greenberg, human beings have developed an elaborate set of unconscious defenses to manage the terror of death. The main defense is our cultural worldview. Christian culture, for instance, generally teaches that God created us and endowed us with the ability to choose between good and evil actions, and that if we choose the good ones, we'll end up in heaven. If you were raised in this tradition, you were taught that, provided you live up to cultural standards of behavior, you will live forever.

It's strange to think about, but one of the main benefits of our culture may be its ability to reassure us that we'll live on after we die. Even secular culture—the culture of consumerism that we all share whether we like it or not—provides us with the possibility of *symbolic* immortality, in such forms as the legacy we leave, the businesses we build, the works of art we create, and the children we raise. So our culture can reduce death anxiety by offering us immortality, with only the caveat that we must live up to its standards. To the extent that we do what we're supposed to do—amass accomplishments, approval, status, or money—we'll live on, in one form or another. We're able to say to ourselves, "I'm such a good person/I'm doing such good things/ I'm leaving such a good legacy/I'm so respected by others, surely I'm not like those people who die young or die suddenly." Yes, it's not totally logical, but neither are human beings. Nonetheless, it has a kind of logic of the heart, which may be enough to distract us from the terror of an impending end.

According to research, this death denial can have serious consequences. For one, we become very tied to our cultural worldview. If I'm relying on my cultural belief in an afterlife, for instance, to protect me from the full emotional realization that I am destined to die, then anything that could undermine that worldview is a potential threat. This idea led researchers to hypothesize that when people are reminded of death, even in a fairly casual way, they should be more likely both to strongly endorse their own culture's worldview and to denigrate people of other cultures. In other words, they should become more prejudiced.

In 2005, German psychologists Eva Jonas and Immo Fritsche joined forces with terror management theory creator Jeff Greenberg to publish a fascinating study addressing this issue in the *Journal of Economic Psychology*. In the city of Magdeburg, Germany, they randomly stopped pedestrians to ask them questions about their beliefs. Although they told participants that they were surveying people's "consumption and television behavior," they slipped in a number of questions about people's belief in the superiority of German culture—questions about how much they would prefer German cars to foreign cars, to what degree they thought Germans were more handsome than foreigners, and how much they would prefer German food to foreign food, among others. Here's the interesting part: they stopped half the study's participants in a small shopping area and the other half directly in front of a cemetery. Presumably, standing in front of a cemetery would, on some level, remind the respondents of death—a condition that the researchers call mortality salience. There was no other difference between these two groups except the fact that one happened to be walking past a cemetery. The results showed that participants who were surveyed in the shopping area liked the German and non-German items approximately equally. Amazingly, however, those surveyed in front of the cemetery displayed greater liking for the German items as well as a decreased liking for the non-German ones.

By the way, results like these aren't limited to Germany. Similar tendencies have been demonstrated in France, India, Italy, Japan, Spain, the United States, and other countries. It's not about being German; it's about being human. It's also important to note that all of this seems to occur unconsciously and automatically, so most of the research participants probably weren't aware they were showing this tendency.

Because these death-denying defenses are unconscious, you may find yourself doubting they're real. It all sounds pretty fanciful. But ask yourself: even after reading the words foretelling your own personal doom in the last few pages, why are you not overwhelmed by terror right now?

We avoid the terror of our demise in another interesting way, says a man who knows a thing or two about the fear of death. Film director John Carpenter says we play with it.

With his vivid white hair and a stare that suggests he can peer into our hearts to find our deepest terrors, Carpenter has creatively birthed some of our most iconic bringers of death, from *Halloween*'s mass-murdering psychopath, Michael Myers, to *The Thing*'s alien shape-shifter. After directing and producing horror films for more than thirty years, he's noticed a kind of paradox.

"We fear death and yet we love to let it entertain us," Carpenter says, and suggests some clear reasons for this. "It's therapeutic. The one thing we fear more than death is *thinking* about death. So, instead, we think about death while we're safely removed from it. We've always used modern myths and stories to explain the world. Monsters are an interesting creation. They're very ancient. In these stories, death is several things at once: the *other*, the *beast*, and the *creature*, the *us*. All of these myths and stories that we pass around help us deal with and understand it."

He makes an interesting point. Have you ever noticed that after a big scream, theatergoers laugh? These forms of entertainment allow us to fool ourselves into thinking death is something safe and they distance us from our own mortality. This may be related to a mechanism that psychologists call, simply, nervous laughter, which happens when we encounter stress. Physician Alex Lickerman of the University of Chicago submits that nervous laughter is a defense mechanism that guards against overwhelming anxiety. "Being able to laugh at a trauma at the moment it occurs, or soon after, signals both to ourselves and others that we believe in our ability to endure it (which is perhaps what makes laughter such a universally pleasurable experience: it makes us feel that everything will be all right)," he writes in *Psychology Today*.

We may laugh because it gives us a sort of symbolic control over death. "Films, especially horror films, invite us to invest in the story by asking us to project ourselves onto the screen," says John Carpenter. "But we, the viewers, always come back to our seats alive. We've beaten death. For most of us, death remains an abstraction."

As long as we keep death an abstraction, we can go about confidently living our lives as though we have all the time in the world to chase opportunity, something Paul Watkins had counted on throughout his youth.

Thinking back on his late teens, Paul Watkins recalls wanting to do something meaningful with his life. What this meant, exactly, remained elusive. His interests were numerous and somewhat generic. He considered a life in academia, in management, in something entrepreneurial. At Tulane University he floated the idea of majoring in history, business administration, and public health before landing on a broad liberal arts degree. It was "essentially as noncommittal as you could get," Paul says.

These career changes were what his friend, a pilot named David Charlebois, might call midflight course corrections. Paul would spend years studying for one career, then change his mind completely. He earned four degrees. He even flirted with the idea of becoming a priest. In fact, he took religious vows. But doubts weighed on him. An entire life surrendered to God sounded noble, but it just seemed to require too many sacrifices.

So, in 1993, Paul headed to the Darden School of Business at the University of Virginia. Over dinner one night, he found himself examining a box of jambalaya mix. "I said to myself, these guys could use some marketing help!" The next day, he called an 800 number on the box and reached the corporate headquarters of Louisiana Gourmet Enterprises Inc. Before he knew it, he had a summer internship. In corporate culture, value was measured in terms of accomplishment and promotion. There was a straightforward path to success. Paul thrived in this environment. The internship eventually became a full-time job. Within one year, the company promoted him to vice president of marketing.

Paul opened a bank account and could now afford his own apartment. He watched with awe as opportunities expanded before him. His responsibilities grew beyond marketing and extended into distribution and manufacturing. Meanwhile, he was learning everything he could about running factories, managing technologies, and overseeing operations. His savings account grew from a few hundred dollars to a couple of thousand. Then to ten thousand dollars. Then twenty thousand.

Louisiana Gourmet Enterprises Inc. was a relatively small company, and when Paul was made CEO in his mid-thirties, he knew his growth opportunities had just about capped out. He began fantasizing about running his own food business. He initially thought it was too ambitious an idea for a young man right out of business school to take on. *Then again*, he thought, *why not try?*

Paul resigned from Louisiana Gourmet Enterprises in late 1996, and took the small amount of capital he'd saved to found Boudreaux's Foods. "The name was purely a marketing decision. I chose it because it's the most common Cajun surname I could think of at the time," he says. "I only had three products: shrimp and crab gumbo, shrimp étouffée, and shrimp Creole. I was nervous. I wasn't sure what I was doing, but I had a good head on my shoulders." His doubts disappeared when he calculated his first-year revenue at a half million dollars. "But if I was going to ever make real money, I needed more products. I made a resolution to scale up the next year. I started looking for opportunities to expand."

He didn't have to go far. He was wandering the grocery store aisles one day, admiring his products on the shelves, when he came across a small self-published diet book called *Sugar Busters*. The authors were a group of local medical doctors and a businessman. Paul approached them with an offer to develop, market, and sell a whole line of food products under a licensing arrangement and to bring them on as partners, to which they agreed.

Years passed. Paul went from producing just three products to producing forty-seven—everything from mayonnaise and salad dressings, to bread, sports drinks, and pastas. He was happy, rich, and successful. Paul Watkins had everything that, externally at least, should have made him happy.

———

Although each of us is unique, we all exist in cultural contexts that tell us what's valuable. Pervasive messages that come across our television and computer screens, through our radio speakers, and on roadside billboards convey very clearly what is valued—the clothes we wear, the cars we drive, the status of our jobs, the size of our homes and of our waistlines. Even those of us who actively resist such messages can't help but feel, on some level, that these external trappings measure our value. There is no dearth of people who, in fact, judge us in this way. Of course, all these trappings cost money.

In his book *Escape from Evil*, the great cultural anthropologist Ernest Becker writes that money "buys bodyguards, bullet-proof glass, and better medical care. Most of all it can be passed on, and so radiates its powers even after death, giving one a semblance of immortality." Money is one of the most obvious external measures of how we live up to our culture's standards. According to terror management theorists Solomon, Pyszczynski, and Greenberg, the accumulation of wealth should thus serve a key role in distracting and protecting us from the fear of our impending death.

If this sounds fanciful, consider the message that President George W. Bush delivered after the events of September 11, 2001, perhaps the American people's most significant reminder of their fragile mortality since the nation's founding. You might expect the president to urge people to care for one another, for their families and neighbors, and to keep faith in their government and the power of justice. Without an understanding of terror management theory, however, you might have found it surprising that he urged Americans to shop. "We cannot let the terrorists achieve the objective of frightening our nation to the point where we don't do business, where people don't shop," President Bush urged. "Mrs. Bush and I want to encourage Americans to go out shopping." And that's exactly what Americans did during the next three months. The U.S. Commerce Department reported an increase in consumer spending of more than 6 percent from October to December of 2001, the strongest pace in four years.

Research by psychologists Tim Kasser of Knox College and Kennon Sheldon of the University of Missouri provides data supporting these observations. The researchers asked college students to imagine what their financial standing would be in fifteen years, including their salary; the value of their homes, cars, and investments; and the amount of money they would spend on entertainment, leisure activities, and clothing. But before they answered these questions, they asked half the participants to ponder their mortality by writing a paragraph or two about their thoughts and feelings regarding their deaths. By now you shouldn't be surprised to hear that the students who wrote about their deaths said they planned to be worth more financially and spend more money on luxury items than did those who hadn't pondered their mortality.

Although none of these students knew it, they may have been using expectations of their material wealth to defend against the unpleasant emotions generated by writing about their mortality. The unconscious logic goes something like "If I'm rich, I don't have to worry about it." It's comforting and distracting to think about one's material wealth and future status, and this may have served to reassure these students that there was no danger of their dying—at least not for a very long time.

Viewed through this lens, financial success such as that Paul Watkins experienced during much of his life exerts a powerful draw upon people because it allows us to feel special, as if we're going to live forever. But such fragile logic may have limits, particularly when we are reminded of death in a way that defies all our mechanisms of denial and defense. Ultimately, death isn't a two-paragraph essay; nor is it a television report of tragedy at a distance—even when that tragedy is as terrible as 9/11. Sometimes death strikes much closer to home.

———

On a Tuesday morning in September of 2001, Paul was startled awake by a phone call. His head felt heavy, his body sluggish, as he answered the phone. "Paul, turn on the TV," boomed the voice of his office manager.

He stumbled out of bed and rubbed his eyes. "Which channel?"

"It doesn't matter."

Like the rest of the world, Paul tuned into an alien scene of the familiar New York City skyline obscured by dense black smoke and of the Pentagon burning in Arlington, Virginia. "People kept talking about airplanes being taken over by hijackers. Everyone was talking about the passengers and the people in the buildings. Suddenly I was thinking about the pilots."

Not just any pilot, but a friend of his. Paul had last seen David Charlebois that past July, at a house a short bike ride from Rehoboth Beach in Delaware. David was a neat and entertaining guy a few years younger than Paul. He and Paul got together with their mutual friends whenever Paul was out east on a business trip and David wasn't flying for American Airlines. That July evening, David had talked about a scrappy little dog he'd recently adopted named Chance.

"There were thousands of pilots in the air on 9/11. The odds were really small that David was on one of the hijacked planes," Paul says.

But when he tried David's cell phone, it went straight to voice mail. Paul was worried. A couple of hours later, his phone rang.

It was a mutual friend, and his tone of voice said it all. Paul's heart sank.

David was the first officer on American Airlines Flight 77. At 9:37 that morning, it had slammed into the western side of the Pentagon.

———

The house on Marigny Street in New Orleans reminded Candy Chang of death. Its darkened windows were busted out. The blue-tinged wood siding was peeling. Inside the house, the rafters were exposed like bones. To keep out squatters, the sides had been completely boarded up, making people inside feel as if they were encased in a coffin.

The district had seen its share of decline since the floods of Hurricane Katrina, but it was coming back with a resurgence of music venues, lively restaurants, and a wave of new artists such as Candy Chang, who had moved into the neighborhood of narrow shotgun houses in 2010. She'd discovered the eccentricities of the community: the man blowing a trumpet on a street corner, the neighbor building a mystery space machine on another. "It feels like it was drawn by a five-year-old, in the very best way," Candy says.

Chang, a young Taiwanese American designer and urban planner, was working in Finland when she learned that a close friend and mentor of hers had died unexpectedly. "It made me think about what's really important to me in my life," she says. "Death is something we're often discouraged to talk about or even think about: 'Don't go there. It's too sad. You don't need to think about it until you're older.' Maybe that's why it took me so long to lean into those thoughts, but when I finally did, I found a deep comfort and clarity I didn't expect."

Not long after her friend's death, she followed an unrealized dream and moved to New Orleans, home of some of the most beautiful houses and buildings she'd ever seen. But it also had one of the highest numbers of abandoned properties in America. Candy lived about a mile from the most dilapidated house in the neighborhood. "It looked like something out of a horror movie," she remembers.

Like director John Carpenter, Candy saw an opportunity to play with death. One February morning, she pulled on a sweater and jeans, bought a big cup of coffee from a local café, and crossed town, fully prepared to do something bold. At Burgundy Street, she stopped at a corner and gazed at the abandoned, orange-roofed house with determination. Four friends were waiting for her there with buckets of black chalkboard paint, paint rollers, brushes, a stencil, metal chalk holders, and gloves. Together, they laid some butcher paper and trash bags along the sidewalk to form a tarp. The chilled morning air was warming quickly as they started painting the side of the house with primer. An old man on a bicycle stopped and chatted with Candy about the history of the block. People walking their dogs paused to ask what they were doing. The head of the neighborhood association's anti-blight committee brought Candy and her friends a platter of tea and cookies. A guy in a pirate suit on his way to work at a pirate-themed bar in the French Quarter wandered over and told them some jokes. It was for many just another day in the neighborhood. But not for Candy.

When the primer was dry, she rolled blackboard paint along the entire side of the boarded-up house. At the top, she used stencils to paint in large, bold white letters the words "Before I Die . . ." and beneath that, in much smaller letters, she stenciled the simple phrase "Before I die, I want to _____," roughly eighty times. At one end of the wall, she left a little tray of blue, white, and canary yellow chalk.

"The idea came to me because I felt public spaces are our shared spaces, and they have the power to snap us out of our routines and restore our profound appreciation of what it means to be alive," says Candy.

Before she had even packed up her supplies, people walking by asked if they could write on the wall. A man wrote, "Before I die I want to see my daughter graduate." A couple wrote, "Before I die I want to finish school" and "Before I die I want to go 200 mph." The guy in the pirate outfit wrote, "Before I die I want to be tried for piracy."

Candy didn't know what effect her art project would ultimately have on people. She hoped it would at least make some people stop and think about how short and precious life was. But the street didn't have that much foot traffic. It was more likely that her work would just get spray-painted over by gangs that night.

So Candy was blown away the next morning to see that all eighty lines had been filled in, with responses spilling into the margins. The messages were thoughtful, funny, poetic, and even heartbreaking. Before I die I want to . . . "sing for millions" . . . "hold her one more time" . . . "see my daughter graduate" . . . "abandon all insecurities" . . . "plant a tree" . . . "straddle the International Date Line" . . . "get clean" . . . "live off the grid" . . . "build a school" . . . "be completely myself" . . .

Chang erased that day's chalk contributions only to find the wall repopulated a day later. She posted a few photos of the wall online, and they went viral. Her in-box filled up with earnest messages from students, widowers, business owners, activists, neighborhood leaders, and friends—all who wanted to make a wall in their communities. Today more than a hundred "Before I Die" walls have been created in more than ten languages and twenty-five countries, including Argentina, China, Denmark, Italy, Kazakhstan, Portugal, and South Africa.

Chang's exploration of death had tapped a nerve. For the millions who survive a trauma in their lifetime, the writing's on the wall: life is short. A near-death experience or, in Chang's case, the sudden, unexpected death of a loved one has a particular way of bringing that message home.

Chang wondered if reflecting on death and mortality might lead to powerful benefits. Perhaps a nine-foot white-on-black sign begging the completion of the statement "Before I Die . . ." is the wake-up call we need to see the value in living for today. What if such a message got people to help others more, to give more to charity, to reconsider and reform their life goals, and even to experience better overall mental health?

In their honest encounter with death, more people might take on the qualities of supersurvivors.

———

Paul rode in a car along Maryland Interstate 95. His and David Charlebois's good friend Michael Walker, also a pilot, was driving. It was November 2001. The snow on the ground was thawing. Overhead, big black birds were settled on the power lines. The car exited the interstate and pulled into the tiny parking lot of a flat, gray federal building. Paul buttoned his overcoat against the gloom and the cold. Inside, he and Michael passed through a security checkpoint and entered a small lobby, where an official handed Paul an urn containing the ashes of their friend David.

It was hard to believe David was really gone. "I was stunned and saddened. He was one of the nicest people you'd ever meet: friendly, popular, a genuinely good person. He had a family who loved him." More than a decade after his death, Paul Watkins's words still hang heavy. "It got me thinking. This young man. He was younger than I was. Gosh."

It wasn't that before David was killed Paul was ignorant of death. It was just that before David's death, Paul didn't really see death as something worth spending time thinking about. Life seemed long; certainly long enough for Paul to have made a succession of life choices. He always assumed life would just keep going. This hopping from life path to life path had paid off in remarkable ways. Eventually, after years of searching for his place in the world, he was finally happy.

Or, at least, he had been happy until now.

The drive back from the federal building to Front Royal, Virginia, was solemn. Paul and Michael turned off Highway 66 and drove to a little town on the edge of the Shenandoah River. The Blue Ridge Mountains were covered in white. Down East Criser Road, they passed a library and a grocery store and turned toward Warren Street, past small shops selling Civil War paraphernalia. They eventually arrived at the home of David's parents and solemnly delivered his ashes.

That evening, Paul made himself a cup of coffee and took off his shoes. He didn't sleep that night. "I thought a lot about life. How precious and tenuous life is," he says. "Culture teaches us to expect that we're going to live into our seventies and eighties. Sometimes that happens, sometimes that doesn't. I think people feel they are entitled to that, that they have a right to that. That happens for a lot of people, but not to a fair number of people." If he had been the one who died on September 11 instead of David, Paul wondered if he could honestly say he'd done everything he wanted to do in life.

————

We've seen evidence of how people clothe themselves in the armor of their cultural worldview as a defense against truly realizing they will die. In general, the participants in Solomon, Pyszczynski, and Greenberg's studies didn't consciously know that were marshaling such defenses. If you'd asked them, they'd likely have denied feeling much fear about death. "Yeah, I know it'll happen eventually," they might have said, "but I don't have to worry about that for a long, long time." This certainly was Paul Watkins's refrain as he built his highly lucrative, highly respectable career. On some level, he knew that what he was doing ultimately wasn't meaningful to him. Even though he was enjoying himself, making money, and benefiting from the respect of those around him, somehow it seemed empty. But there would always be tomorrow—after he accumulated his fortune and built his gumbo empire—to do something more meaningful. Life seemed endlessly long—until his friend David died and Paul could no longer deny that life was fragile, and shorter than any of us like to think.

What allowed Paul to confront death honestly while so many others seem to remain in denial? For that matter, why did Candy Chang's "Before I Die" wall affect people differently from John Carpenter's horror films? Shouldn't both reminders of death trigger our tendency toward protective denial?

University of Minnesota psychology researcher Philip Cozzolino has some ideas about this. "The notion that human mortality provides sweetness to life—an added zest that makes living more meaningful—is certainly not the view of death espoused by typical individuals," he writes in his 2006 article in the journal *Psychological Inquiry*. "The more common human response to mortality is likely to involve themes of denial, fear, and/or discomfort." But this very book is filled with cases of people staring death in the face without flinching, and then using the experience as a springboard not into prejudice, materialism, or culturally sanctioned superficial achievements, but into an authentic life governed by their internal compasses.

Cozzolino proposes what he calls *dual-existential systems*. We can encounter death in two distinct ways. One is the superficial, abstract way we bump into it on a daily basis—the glorified but cartoony killing in Hollywood blockbusters and even the real but distant tragedies we see in the news. Cozzolino also thinks this superficial awareness of mortality is what participants in terror management experiments experience. "Terror management theory researchers have made mortality salient for participants by exposing them to generic, abstract representations of death such as gory video scenes, visits to funeral homes," he writes. "Conversely, for a terminal cancer patient or for a person who believes that he or she has actually died in a car crash and come back from the other side, the subject of mortality has become a tangible, experiential fact of life that is systematically integrated into their thoughts and behaviors." He calls this deeper, personal, undeniable encounter with mortality death reflection, and contrasts it with the more superficial, abstract, easily deniable experience of mortality salience.

To prove his point, Cozzolino, along with researchers Angela Staples, Lawrence Meyers, and Jamie Samboceti, performed a series of experiments of the sort that terror management theorists are famous for, but they asked participants to reflect upon death in a way that made it more deeply personal than in past studies. The researchers not only asked participants to imagine their deaths, but also prompted them, among other things, to reflect on the life they had led up to that point. It's reminiscent of the way some survivors of near-death experiences say their lives flash before them, or the question Candy Chang asked passersby to consider. As a result, participants who normally were oriented toward extrinsic ends (e.g., money and fame) but who deeply reflected on their own eventual deaths became less greedy and more spiritual. Interestingly, those who considered death more superficially—those who experienced mortality salience rather than death reflection—became greedier. One of the participants in Cozzolino's research, recalling what it was like to reflect deeply upon death, summed it up well: "I realize now that our time here is relatively short and it makes me want to live my life to the fullest. It seems like such a waste of precious time to become caught up in materialistic modes of thinking."

Of course, life doesn't afford us many opportunities to encounter the idea of death deeply. And when it does, these reflections are typically not pleasant—in fact, they're often traumatic.

———

The morning David Charlebois was killed, people all over the world simultaneously became trauma survivors. Even though most people didn't know someone directly who died in the 9/11 terrorist attacks, many experienced trauma on a vicarious level.

Surveying a sample of American college students, Georg E. Matt of San Diego State University and Carmelo Vázquez of Universidad

Complutense de Madrid found that between 30 and 40 percent of people reported posttraumatic stress and general psychological distress in the weeks following September 11, 2001, even though they were nowhere near the attacks. There were similar findings following the March 11, 2004, train bombings in Madrid that resulted in the largest loss of life from a single terrorist attack in European history.

But people experienced the events of 9/11 in both of the ways explored by Phillip Cozzolino. For most, the attacks were something that happened at a distance. Though the events were very real, for this group of people the actual experience was framed by the borders of a television screen. It wasn't truly personal in the way it was for many others—those who were standing on Church Street or Liberty Street or Vesey Street that day, those who lost someone in the smoldering ruins, or those who narrowly escaped death themselves. The first group of people may have been able to use unconscious terror management defenses to deny their own fear of death. As the theory might predict, perhaps this is why news reports from all over the country highlighted rising prejudice against foreigners as many Americans fled to their own cultural worldviews as a defense mechanism. But people in the second group, such as Paul Watkins, who personally and deeply encountered death, couldn't reassure themselves quite so easily. Many found themselves reexamining their lives. New Yorkers will tell you that their city was transformed in the weeks and months following the attacks. People were talking to each other differently. They were more courteous, more patient, more loving, more generous.

Paul couldn't stop thinking about the course his life had taken. For the first time in years, he wondered why he'd chosen a life in business instead of fulfilling his religious vows. It was hard to remember. Something about ambition and age. He was now forty. His friends were making money, living conventional lives—the kind of lives that had previously seemed to Paul like the right way to live. But had he found real personal meaning in this kind of life, beyond the superficial trappings that only days before had seemed so important?

Since the tragic deaths of David and so many others, Paul realized on an emotional level what he had understood only in a hypothetical way before: We have only a limited amount of time before we die, and there's nothing to do but make the most meaningful choices possible. Society tells us what the valued life paths are, what it takes to be respected by others. Starting his company was one of them, and it seemed easy to follow this path. But things had clearly changed.

Now Paul searched his heart furiously for a more authentic path, and saw that it had been there the whole time.

So he moved out of his upscale apartment and gave away most of his possessions to live in the community at St. Anthony of Padua Priory on Canal Street in New Orleans, joining the Dominican Order of priests. He surrendered his existence to God and committed himself to the ideologies of charity, community, common prayer, study, and service for the rest of his life.

He now sees this transformation as a kind of grace, one that allows him the opportunity to help others. Paul the millionaire entrepreneur had had no way to talk about grace or about God being present in the face of the evil of 9/11. "I couldn't help anybody," he says. "I had silenced myself." His true aspirations had been present all along, concealed by convention and a straightforward view of success. "I felt there was a part of me that I had ignored and hidden from all this time."

In 2005, Paul became the parochial vicar of St. Dominic Parish in New Orleans. Three weeks later, Hurricane Katrina made landfall. The nearby Seventeenth Street Canal levee failed. Garbage-filled water rushed over the city. Paul's Bible and a rosary given to him by his father were lost in the flood.

The priests of St. Dominic Parish were among the last to leave the city during the forced evacuation, and Paul was the very first of them to return. He found the church, as big as an airplane hangar, submerged in ten feet of black water. The pews and kneelers were embedded in mud, and floodwaters had toppled the altar.

The neighborhood remained empty for weeks. Every house was damaged or destroyed. Electricity remained out, and basic resources were scarce. The community was uninhabitable. Paul assessed the ruins and wondered how on earth any neighborhood could come back from this.

But it would come back, and Paul would give it a push. "Someone had to take the risk and start rebuilding first," he says. "The priests came back, and we all started cleaning. The National Guard carried out the pews. We reopened the parish and the schools, even though no one was there to use them. It was part of the healing process for the people, to see the church getting back to working condition. To have the church make a statement that it was committed to the city and the parish gave people hope."

But to Paul's surprise, the neighborhoods didn't just bounce back; in many ways they bounced forward, in supersurvivor fashion. "If you're going to reorient your personal values after a big tragedy like this, eventually you're going to reorient your community's values, which is what happened," Paul says. "There's no doubt the storm changed the city. There's more compassion among the people. The focus on faith changed. It got stronger. Today, people who never, ever considered coming to New Orleans are moving here, and the city welcomes them."

And in a weird convergence of faith and synchronicity, one of those newcomers was a young artist named Candy Chang. She'd come to New Orleans mourning the death of a dear friend.

Several weeks later, she would haul buckets of chalkboard paint to a dilapidated house with orange roof trim and stencil the words "Before I Die . . ."

7

Faith's Mixed Blessing

Here is my secret. It is very simple: It is only with
the heart that one can see rightly; what is essential
is invisible to the eye.
—ANTOINE DE SAINT-EXUPÉRY, *THE LITTLE PRINCE*

The dramatic conversion of James Cameron from schoolboy to supersurvivor began in the foreboding darkness of a hot Indiana night in August 1930. James was known in Marion as an amiable and upstanding kid who worked at the Adams Street interurban train station shining white peoples' shoes. Unlike James, his school friends Thomas Shipp and Abe Smith had no compunction about committing petty (and not so petty) crimes. All three boys were in Thomas's convertible coupe coming back from tossing horseshoes in a pal's backyard when Abe suddenly pulled out a .38-caliber Iver Johnson special from his overalls. "Let's go rob somebody," he said with a crazed look in his eyes. "I'll be the leader, and you boys'll be my gang."

Being the youngest of the three, of small stature for sixteen, and a natural follower, James wasn't sure how he could back out of what he feared was about to happen. They crossed the Thirty-Eighth Street Bridge out of town, and before long they were cruising down a shadowy country road. Abe raised his hand, signaling to Thomas to apply the brakes. He'd spotted a Buick pulled over in a wooded area by the river.

James followed them out into the woods on foot, hanging back a little as they waded into knee-high grass awash in pale moonlight. A few yards ahead was the Buick, parked by the muddy river snaking past the Marion glass factory. A man and woman were inside talking. Abe shoved something into James's hand and flashed a threatening glance.

"There's nothing to it," he said. "Just take this gun and put it on the people. Then say, 'Stick 'em up.'"

James's stomach tightened. He knew that what Abe was telling him to do was wrong; he felt it in every bone of his body. He thought about his God-fearing mother waiting for him back at home and suddenly wanted more than anything to drop the gun and run to her. But he was afraid of what Abe would do. Abe was his friend, yes, but James had come to fear him. The older boy could be cruel, vindictive, and unpredictable; James didn't want to trigger his anger. Every step toward the car felt more and more wrong. Years later he would wonder what went awry in his boyhood mind to keep him from summoning the courage to turn around. But for whatever reason, he didn't, and regret for this would later consume him.

James yanked the car door open.

"What's going on!" the man inside demanded, wide-eyed and confused.

James leveled the gun at him. His heart was racing. "Get your hands up!" He nearly shrieked the order, his voice struggling to find a register of authority. Puberty had not yet fully changed his voice.

Abe stepped up, knowing that James's fearful and guilty look would get them nowhere. "Out of the car," he ordered the couple. "Keep your hands high!"

Just then, James realized something that made his whole body go cold. The man he was holding up was Claude Deeter, one of his best customers from the train station. Claude was a good man.

James was thinking sensibly again. He shoved the gun back at Abe. "I want nothing to do with this." The boys didn't even try to stop him. They let him run off into the darkness. By the time James reached the country road, his skin was crawling with sweat and his heart was sinking with an understanding of what he had done. He thought about going to the police, turning his friends in. But in Indiana at the dawn of the 1930s, everyone knew what "justice" meant for black kids. Besides, he reassured himself, Abe and Thomas would just take a few dollars. Everything would be all right.

The Thirty-Eighth Street Bridge appeared around the bend. He was about to cross it when three gunshots rang out from the distance.

James didn't know it, but Claude Deeter had been shot. As he lay dying in the hospital, Claude pointed investigators to the boys. It didn't take long for police cruisers to surround James's mother's house. They found the boy hiding under his bedsheets and arrested him. As they pushed him outside, James heard his mother cry out, "Lord, have mercy. Give me strength, dear Jesus!"

Throughout Indiana over the next twelve hours there was talk about lynching the prisoners. At that time in history, justice for black people didn't always involve courtrooms, judges, juries of one's peers, or even prison sentences. Sometimes it involved brutal summary executions at the hands of angry white mobs. Between 1882 and the rise of the civil rights movement of the late 1960s, roughly thirty-five hundred black people were lynched in the United States. Less than a day after Abe and Thomas killed Claude Deeter, the surging, roiling sound of bedlam rose from outside James's jailhouse cell. A mob had surrounded the jail entrance, ropes in hand. According to some reports, the Ku Klux Klan was responsible for stirring the crowd's anger. Despite attempts by the police to prevent people from breaching the jail, two men used sledgehammers to break down the jailhouse door. The mob flooded into the building. Shouts of racial epithets could be heard over the slamming of footsteps. Blood for blood is all the crowd would accept.

Dragging Thomas Shipp out into the balmy night, punching and kicking him, the mob strung him up by the neck from the bars of a jail window. They took Abe next, pulling him across the street to the looming courthouse through a gauntlet of fists, boot heels, and bats. They shoved his head through a noose and hoisted his body from a maple tree. Abe wrested his hands free and pulled up on the rope that was strangling him, to catch his breath.

From his cell, James watched in horror as the mob let Abe down from the tree long enough to break both his arms with bats and then pull him back up by his neck. When Abe was dead, a group retrieved Thomas's body from the jailhouse window and strung him up next to Abe from the maple tree. A studio photographer was called to capture the moment. The photographer took his time setting up the shot, angling the floodlights on the tree to illuminate the bodies properly in the gathering darkness.

James thought about the crime he had been involved in perpetrating. He wondered what would have happened if he had turned in Abe and Thomas peacefully when he had the chance. Maybe he should have stood up to them instead of running away. Now three people were dead, and the mob was coming back for more. Maybe this was his fault, he thought for a moment. Maybe he deserved to die.

Then the crowd came for James. Beating him into surrender until blood ran down his face, washed away only by his tears, the mob hauled him into the town square. Someone smacked his head with the end of a pick. Fists, rocks, and spit pummeled him. He recognized faces in the rabble, people he knew, people he liked, people who he thought were fond of him. James was no longer a human being to them, but a nameless proxy, an emblem that would come to instill fear into a subjugated black community. At the courthouse maple tree, a loop of rope as thick as his thumb was fastened under James's jaw. He looked out into a pitiless crowd. As the noose tightened around his neck, he heard something strange.

A lone voice, soft and indecipherable at first, pacified the crowd. Within moments, the rope went slack and a hush came over the mob.

Of the many archived newspaper reports of the famous Marion lynching of August 7, 1930, none provides any reason for the mob's letting James go. In the years that followed, some speculated it was the sheriff who talked some reason into the hangmen. Others suggested that the mob took pity on James because he looked so young and was lighter-skinned than Thomas or Abe. The voice that said, "Take this boy back. He had nothing to do with any raping or killing," might have belonged to one of Deeter's family members, pleading to end the bloodshed. Or perhaps the mob's adrenaline had simply waned.

But until the great civil rights activist Dr. James Cameron, a supersurvivor who went on to shape history for the better, died in 2006 at the age of ninety-two, he would swear it was the voice of God that pacified the crowd and saved him that night.

———

Some may question whether James Cameron should be considered a supersurvivor. After all, he wasn't a totally innocent person, though he never claimed he was. He was flawed, and he played a role in wrongdoings that culminated in the death of a good man at the bloody hands of people James probably shouldn't have considered "friends." But nothing about supersurvival requires that a person's past be morally spotless. Unlike with many survivors in this book, James's trauma resulted from a chain of events set in motion partially by his own actions. But if it were necessary to be a saint to be a supersurvivor, virtually no one would have a chance. As we've seen time and time again, however, trauma can sometimes turn lives around. For James, that night in 1930 began a journey, one guided by his conviction that God had saved him.

Nobody will ever truly know, of course, if the hand of God was at work. Philosophers and theologians have debated the existence and nature of God for millennia. René Descartes and Thomas Aquinas thought they could prove that God existed; Bertrand Russell and Richard Dawkins were pretty sure they could disprove this—or at least cast considerable doubt on it. The debate rages on, with no end in sight.

Fortunately, it isn't necessary to know whether the divine exists to investigate the effects of faith. In his perhaps most controversial work, *The Future of an Illusion*, infamous critic of religion Sigmund Freud writes about his approach to religious beliefs: "Of the reality of most of them we cannot judge; just as they cannot be proved, neither can they be refuted." Yet Freud nonetheless studied closely what he believed were the ill effects of believing in a god.

But Freud's methods were crude, consisting primarily of in-depth case studies, often of himself or his emotionally troubled patients. Though respected by some, his work is hardly considered conclusive by today's scientific standards. Since 1927, when *The Future of an Illusion* was published, social scientists have birthed countless studies trying to answer the question "What good is faith?"

Many have famously shown benefits of aspects of faith. Most significant in its scope is the research, spearheaded by David Snowdon, that has come to be known as the Nun Study. As an epidemiologist and professor of neurology at the University of Kentucky, Snowdon was initially interested in what factors would increase or decrease the risk of Alzheimer's disease. More than twenty-five years and fifty published research articles later, the study ended up being so much more. His research team followed about seven hundred American Catholic nuns of the School Sisters of Notre Dame as they aged. Examining them annually, the team collected information on cognitive and physical functioning, medical diseases, genetics, and nutrition. Detailed records kept by the sisters on virtually every stage of their lives also meant that researchers could determine earlier risk and protective factors with a great degree of accuracy.

The most trumpeted finding of the study was a simple one: happier nuns live longer. In 1930, when the nuns were only about twenty-two years old on average, the Mother Superior asked each of them to write an autobiography. By the late 1990s, about a hundred and eighty of these narratives were still in existence. Snowdon, along with researchers Deborah Danner and Wallace Friesen, identified passages in the narratives that referred to emotions, and he counted up the number of positive, negative, and neutral ones.

The number of positive emotions referred to in those early autobiographies actually predicted risk of death six decades later. Perhaps even more astounding, however, was that, as a group, the nuns lived longer than everyone else. In a study published in *The Journals of Gerontology*, Steven Butler and David Snowdon tracked down the records of twenty-five hundred School Sisters of Notre Dame who were born between 1886 and 1916. The researchers were interested in how many of the nuns would pass away between 1965 to 1989 compared to the general population of American women with similar characteristics (e.g., age and race). About a thousand sisters died during that period, making them only 73 percent as likely to have died as a similarly aged American woman during the same years. In fact, according to some statistics, the average life span for a Roman Catholic nun is about eight years longer than that of other American women. This isn't a new insight. In 1959 an article appearing in *Time* magazine titled "Long-Lived Nuns" cited research by University of Dayton sociologist Con Fetcher documenting a higher-than-average longevity for sisters.

But even now the causes of this life span advantage aren't clearly understood. Were researchers seeing the tangible benefits of having faith? "It remains a mystery to me how [so many of] these women have lived a century or longer," Snowdon writes in his 2001 book, *Aging with Grace*. "But as I learned the details of their pasts, as we gathered information about their mental and physical capabilities, as I came to know them as individuals, and as we analyzed their genes and their brains . . . clues to their longevity have begun to emerge.

"Two of these factors cannot be scientifically tested by the Nun Study data," Snowdon admits. "And yet after fifteen years of working with the sisters, I believe strongly in their importance. The first is the deep spirituality these women share. . . . The power of community is the second factor." There could be other factors—the sisters' high level of education, good medical care, high-quality diet, low level of smoking and alcohol consumption, and perhaps even low job stress. This is often the case when studying the physical and psychological health effects of religion—it's almost impossible to tease apart faith from other, more tangible trappings of a spiritual life.

What is clear, at least, is that something about religion can be beneficial to believers. And it's not just about nuns. Dozens of studies have now documented the benefits for laypeople of religion and spirituality in coping with a variety of life stressors, including cancer, heart failure, kidney failure, depression, obesity, serious mental illness, and even the daily hassles of ordinary life.

It's important to mention that nobody is scientifically claiming that being nonreligious is a detriment to one's mental or physical health. However, having a genuine sense of faith appears, in many cases, to be a very good thing. It may even save lives, or at least prolong them a few years, as it did for the School Sisters of Notre Dame. As for James Cameron, while we can debate the likelihood of a true divine intervention saving him from a bloodthirsty lynch mob, his newfound faith would give his life meaning and a new direction that ultimately would make the world a better place.

———

In the city of Anderson, Indiana, James Cameron, now a young man in his early twenties, waited in a small community room filled with empty folding chairs. He wondered if anyone would show up tonight, or if cowardice would once again win the day. The Marion lynching, and the crime in which he had been involved, had shattered everything he thought he knew about life. He had spent a year in jail waiting to go to trial and four long years in prison reconstructing his faith and even figuring out what faith meant now. Whether it was because of God or the sympathies of a seemingly merciless mob, he'd faced certain death and had miraculously, mysteriously survived. For James, exactly how he had survived didn't matter so much as why.

The reason became increasingly simple to him. He felt that God had a mission for him: to turn his suffering, guilt, and anger into something precious—a way of making the world a better place. Perhaps just as mysterious as his survival, James emerged from his experience with a renewed sense of ever-deepening faith.

Personal and historical accounts credit his conversion to Catholicism to a surprising source. As soon as the lynch mob released him, a police cruiser escorted him out of Marion to nearby Anderson for protection. "The sheriff there, he was an important player in this story," says civil rights activist and Cameron scholar Fran Kaplan. "This sheriff's name was Bernard Bradley. He was a kind person. He cared for this boy. The sheriff was a devout Catholic, so he couldn't have been part of the Ku Klux Klan." As James was recovering from his severe beating at the hands of the mob, Sherriff Bradley allowed him to be a trustee of the jail, which meant he could come and go as he wanted while he awaited trial. He even babysat the sheriff's young children. Even after an all-white jury convicted James in 1931 as an accessory before the fact in the murder of Claude Deeter, he and Sheriff Bradley remained close. Bradley died of cancer quite young, but James never forgot his kindness.

Such kindness contrasted starkly with the cruelty that divided America's races. While James went to prison for his part in the crime, the men responsible for the murders of Thomas Shipp and Abe Smith were never brought to justice. Nobody has ever claimed that the two boys were innocent of their crimes, but that didn't give an angry mob the right to execute them without a trial. America was filled with racial prejudice, typified by the lynching of men and boys, but perpetrated on a daily basis in ways far more common and insidious. "I realized I had reached and passed beyond the crisis between light and darkness, between good and evil," James wrote in his autobiography, *A Time of Terror*. His near-death experience and the moment of seeming-divine intervention galvanized his faith and propelled him to act. "I was thankful to God for everything—the trees, the grass, the flowers, the birds of the air, the beasts of the fields, for my worn and torn body, and a sick mind made whole again." James continued: "With faith and prayer over my lips forever, I was determined to keep my hands on the throttle and my eyes upon the rails. . . . I was now a young man, twenty-one years of age, who had time to pick up the loose ends of his life and weave them into something beautiful, worthwhile, and God-like."

He would begin planting the seeds of change by inviting others to join him in creating Anderson's first NAACP chapter. Now he stood in that empty room full of folding chairs, waiting patiently as the hour of the first chapter meeting came and went. "People were afraid to join," Kaplan says. "The perception was that if anyone were to be caught joining the organization, they'd lose their jobs, or worse." But after a while, the first brave people came through the door and filled the folding chairs. James smiled and welcomed them. These early seeds blossomed, and over the next decade, he founded new branches in Muncie and South Bend—and went on to become one of the most promising leaders in the burgeoning civil rights movement of the 1950s.

But it made him a target.

"He wasn't afraid for himself, but he was for his family. He was getting death threats all the time," explains his son, Virgil Cameron. "We were going to move to Canada, but we stopped in Milwaukee on the way, and that's where he decided we'd stay." Milwaukee was a thriving industrial manufacturing town and a perfect place for the Cameron family to settle. For starters, James was able to get a good job at a box factory. Milwaukee also hosted a substantial black community that had come in the Great Migration of millions of African Americans out of the rural South in the early twentieth century. Nationally, the civil rights movement was progressing. By 1955, black leadership was adopting the principles of civil disobedience, and Milwaukee was about to become a big player. For every national demonstration James joined—such as the March on Washington at which Reverend Martin Luther King Jr. gave his "I Have a Dream" speech—he was also on the local frontlines, participating in demonstrations to desegregate urban housing.

Centralizing and binding the fragmented ideologies of the movement were the black churches, including the Catholic church James and his family belonged to. "The emergence of indigenous black institutions in response to societal and governmental repression is perhaps the crowning achievement of black culture. The black church, originally meant to rein in black resistance, became the foundation upon which it was built," writes Lawrence Levine in his book *Black Culture and Black Consciousness*. Inspired by this faith-based movement perpetuated by minister-activists such as the Reverend Martin Luther King Jr., who was leading fair housing marches in Chicago, James joined in landmark demonstrations in support of an open housing bill. After two hundred consecutive days of protest, he, along with thousands of Milwaukee residents, forced the city to desegregate neighborhoods, allowing African Americans the right to own houses anywhere in Milwaukee. In fact, the first federal open housing law was modeled on the one made in Milwaukee.

Virgil Cameron sometimes wonders what kept his father going. No matter what legislation was enacted, there remained the ever-present bigotry no laws could expunge. His father obviously was driven by a strong desire for justice and equal rights. But this was only part of the story. Virgil also says that his father was trying to redeem himself in the eyes of God for the role he had played in the deaths of Claude Deeter, Abe Smith, and Thomas Shipp.

Some may find it counterintuitive that religion was such a motivating factor in James's personal journey toward supersurvival and in the fight for civil rights more broadly. To be sure, it would have been easy for him and other civil rights leaders to conclude that God had it out for them, was indifferent to their plight, or simply didn't exist. After all, wasn't this unjust world ultimately God's creation? As we will see, not every religious believer who encounters trauma holds as steadfastly to faith as James did. Yet for him and his compatriots, every subsequent church bombing, lynching, and hate crime brought about something extraordinary: the power of faith transformed the pain into genuine hope for change. Faith seemed to help people cope and to strive for better days, even when logic dictated the opposite. Faith filled them with the courage to look the reality of racial prejudice in the face without flinching and ask the question "What now?" This courage, combined with the confidence in their personal abilities to make a difference, is what we define in chapters 2 and 3 as grounded hope.

Faith is good—at least it was for James. But we've all heard of people consumed with religion in an unhealthy way—with a faith that torments them, fills them with guilt, or turns them against their friends. This begs a second question: is faith always good?

––––––

In 1959, as the United States experienced widespread civil rights reform, an eleven-year-old named Michael Bussee rode his bicycle to the public library in Riverside, California, in a desperate search for a different kind of change. Recently, his fifth-grade classmates had registered that something was different about Michael and were hurling a terrible-sounding word at him. He didn't know what it meant, but he knew it was something bad. He paused at an index card in the library's card catalog that directed him to books on homosexuality, all of which were shelved under the topic "Abnormal Psychology." *Oh God*, he thought, *it's a real thing*. This word finally explained why he had been developing crushes on other schoolboys.

For Michael, this was a pivotal moment. The beliefs he had been raised with told him that his attractions were wrong, that he suffered from an illness, and that, according to the strictest interpretation of the Bible, homosexuality was a sinful perversion. Homosexuality was not exactly talked about in his church, but even at his young age, Michael had developed an appreciation for its spiritual consequences. If he didn't figure out some way to overcome it, Michael told himself, the Bible laid out the consequences. "First Corinthians, chapter six, verses nine through eleven," recites Michael. " 'Or do you not know that wrongdoers will not inherit the kingdom of God? Do not be deceived: Neither the sexually immoral nor idolaters nor adulterers nor men who have sex with men will inherit the kingdom of God.' "

Over time he grew to hate his romantic feelings toward other men, but the thought of never being loved terrified him. An urgency to save himself from a life of loneliness, so-called depravity, and eternal damnation put him on a desperate path to make himself straight. Michael was going to fight this "illness," and he would spend the next five decades in a dogged attempt to do so.

As a freshman in college, he volunteered to man a crisis hotline at the Melodyland Christian Center megachurch. "Every once in a while people would call in and whisper, 'I have something wrong with me that I can't talk about,' " Michael recalls, "and I knew exactly what they were saying." The way out seemed simple enough: If you were a Christian, you couldn't be homosexual. If you thought otherwise, Satan had misled you. No one was truly homosexual, Michael told himself and his callers. With enough prayer and time, all those feelings would vanish.

Given his success as a hotline counselor, Melodyland Christian Center tasked Michael to help launch its first ministry for gays. He and his cofounders based their so-called "reorientation" or "reparative" therapy on a combination of twelve-step programs, psychotherapy, Bible study, and prayer. "Homosexuality, we felt, was a manifestation of unmet needs," Michael recalls. "If people met these needs in a more spiritually healthy way, their impure feelings would diminish over time. If you had faith and you prayed hard enough, you'd succeed. If it didn't happen, it was because you didn't have enough faith, or you had a sin to confess that's blocking you from God's gift." This is reminiscent of some of the circular logic of the positive thinking movement discussed in chapter 2. Like the paradox of positive thinking, Michael now recognizes that this idea often perpetuated guilt, depression, and self-hatred among the very people he was trying to help. "The implication," he says, "is you might not be a real Christian."

In September of 1976, the church hosted a symposium for ex-gay support groups, which led to the creation of an umbrella organization called Exodus International. This would have been a triumphant day for Michael if not for one very big problem. As a leader and founding member of Exodus, he found that the program he had helped develop to reorient others was not helping him. He was also seeing a disturbing trend among his clients. One man purposely veered his car into a tree. Another was so despondent over his failure to change that he took a razor blade to his genitals and doused his wounds with drain cleaner. Many others fell apart, collapsing under the weight of guilt and self-loathing, and Michael never saw them again. It's what he calls "going underground."

In the years after Michael observed these frightening outcomes, a debate would rage within the mental health field on the effectiveness of sexual reorientation therapy. Though the debate continues to this day, most research has not supported the effectiveness of the therapy, and the entire field is fraught with major methodological flaws. In 2008, Julianne M. Serovich, professor and chair of the Ohio State University's Department of Human Development and Family Science, and a team of colleagues systematically examined twenty-eight research studies on sexual reorientation therapy. In the *Journal of Marital and Family Therapy*, they write that the limitations of this research "include a lack of theory, inconsistent definition and measurement of sexual orientation, restricted samples, lack of longitudinal designs, and sex disparity." Michael's doubts in what he was doing with his clients would be further confirmed by organizations such as the American Psychological Association, the American Psychiatric Association, the American Counseling Association, the American School Counselor Association, the National Association of School Psychologists, and the National Association of Social Workers, all of which have since enacted policies opposing sexual reorientation therapies on the basis that homosexuality is not a mental illness and thus is not something that needs to or can be "cured."

The only thing that kept Michael Bussee going, it seemed, was his friend and Exodus cofounder, Gary Cooper. Wonderfully and disastrously, their close working relationship blossomed into romance.

Gary was a young man with a neat mustache, short hair that fell loosely over his brow, a square chin, and bright eyes. Despite Michael's ever-deepening doubts about Exodus, the two men continued to travel to testify at churches across the country. On a fateful flight together to Indianapolis in 1979, Michael hit a breaking point.

He was reading Glendon Swarthout's novel *Bless the Beasts and Children*, pausing every few pages to recite a passage to Gary, who was in the seat next to him. "It was about misfit boys who eventually break free and band together to find their dignity," remembers Michael. "They grew tired of being thought of as something less. At the end they release a herd of buffalo and set themselves free at the same time. Gary said, 'You know, this kind of relates to us, doesn't it?' I was crying. I told Gary I loved him. He told me he loved me."

This was the first time Michael had ever truly felt love. It was the kind of love he had feared he would never experience, the kind of love he hadn't thought possible for a gay man, the kind of love he had thought he would have to make himself straight in order to find.

But this love carried with it dire consequences. Michael was told by members of the organization that he was now beyond salvation. Some described in scathing detail the flames of hell that were going to consume him in the final days. In 1979, like many of their clients before them, Michael and Gary left Exodus and went underground. Although they were open about their sexuality and their relationship to a small group of friends, they kept their previous involvement in the organization a closely guarded secret.

Michael had become quite adept at concealing himself from others. He felt intensely guilty for his role in what Exodus had done and was continuing to do to gay men just like him, people who just wanted to find the love of God and the love of others. He was full of conflicting thoughts and feelings. Part of him wanted to put religion behind him. *Who needs God, anyway?* he often thought. But he couldn't give up his faith; it wasn't that easy. The truth was, Michael still wondered if being gay was a sin. According to many of his former friends in Exodus, he and Gary were destined for hell. Maybe, he thought, they were right.

Though that frightening thought haunted Michael, he didn't see any alternative. "No matter what," he recalls, "we had to be honest with ourselves, even if that meant an eternity in hell."

———

It seems like a natural human tendency to approach religion as an all-or-nothing proposition. Many say that religion is all good; many claim it's all bad. James Cameron's life and the collective history of the School Sisters of Notre Dame may give the impression that the answer to such questions is simple and positive. But Michael's story presents a very different picture. While his faith served as a kind of beacon throughout his life, guiding his choices just as James's religious convictions had, Michael's beliefs often haunted and disturbed him. For most gay men, the discovery of their sexuality, usually in childhood, is emotionally difficult. With a historical lack of positive role models and a culture often quick to judge, it takes some children years to reach a place of comfort with their sexuality. But Michael's religious beliefs added to this already significant burden, transforming a difficult realization into a traumatic one.

Both James's story of inspiration and Michael's history of misgivings and uncertainty reflect the truth of many people's experiences of faith. For some, religious beliefs and practices are comforting, buffer the damaging effects of trauma, and galvanize personal growth. For others, however, they can be a source of heartbreak.

An increasingly large number of research studies document connections between religious struggle and compromised mental and physical health. For instance, in 2004, chaplain and researcher George Fitchett and his team distributed questionnaires to patients at Rush University Medical Center. Participants with three serious illnesses—diabetes, congestive heart failure, and cancer—completed questionnaires asking about religion, emotional distress, and well-being. Slightly more than half the patients said they experienced no religious conflict or struggle whatsoever, while the remainder indicated some degree of struggle. As expected, those who said they were experiencing religious struggle reported heightened emotional distress and depression. It's important to note that studies like this one can't tell us whether it was religious struggle that caused the emotional distress or the other way around. But it's clear there's a connection.

Struggle with, and even loss of, faith are common in the wake of trauma and adversity, though how common is not fully known. Some studies seem to show that trauma leads a large number of people to give up their faith, whereas other studies show just the opposite, that trauma tends to increase people's faith. A team of researchers headed by Menachem Ben-Ezra of Ariel University Center of Samaria, Israel, surveyed 111 women about their religious beliefs. About half the women had been victims of sexual trauma and half had not. Nonetheless, these two groups were similar in other ways, including age, religion, and marital status. When asked whether they had changed their religious beliefs as a result of the trauma, 45 percent said they hadn't, and a tiny 8 percent said they had become more religious.

In contrast, a full 47 percent said they had become more secular since the trauma. By way of comparison, 25 percent of the nonvictimized women considered themselves nonreligious at the time of the study, compared to a whopping 47 percent of the sexually victimized women.

On the other hand, when Loyola University of Maryland researchers Kari O'Grady, Deborah Rollison, Timothy Hanna, Heidi Schreiber-Pan, and Manuel Ruiz interviewed survivors of 2010's devastating earthquake in Haiti, they found very different results. A full 80 percent of these interviewees agreed or strongly agreed with the statement "My faith in a God/higher power has grown since the earthquake," and 71 percent said they practiced their religion more regularly since the earthquake.

Whether religious faith is strengthened or weakened by trauma probably depends on a complex array of factors, possibly including the type of trauma, the age at which it occurs, and the degree of distress it causes, not to mention possible cultural, socioeconomic, and other demographic influences. It may also depend on the particular content of the person's religious beliefs going into the trauma.

Though most religious Westerners purport to worship the same God, the specifics of their beliefs can differ dramatically. Some people, for instance, view God as merciful and forgiving, whereas others see God as judgmental, a deity who punishes those who do not obey his commandments. The important implications of this particular distinction for how people cope with adversity is dramatically illustrated by a 2011 study published in the *Journal of Behavioral Medicine* by University of Miami psychologist Gail Ironson and her research team. The researchers followed 101 HIV-positive men and women for four years, meeting with them every six months. Participants completed surveys, sat for detailed interviews, and had their blood checked for indicators that the virus might be progressing. They answered questions about everything from health maintenance behaviors to medication adherence, sexual habits, and mental health issues. Participants also told researchers about their personal views of God. The researchers were interested in whether participants' images of God would predict CD4 count (an indication of immune health) and HIV viral load (a measure of the amount of the virus in the bloodstream).

The results were astounding. Those who held a view of God as harsh, judgmental, or punishing, much as Michael had, lost CD4 cells two and a half times faster over the four years of the study than those who didn't share this belief; also, their viral load increased more than three times faster. Because belief that God can be punitive isn't mutually exclusive with a belief that God can be benevolent, it's worth looking at things from a different angle. Those who held a view of God as merciful, benevolent, and forgiving lost CD4 cells five times slower than those who didn't share this belief, and their viral load increased eight and a half times slower.

Of course, it's possible that viral load levels and immune functioning had nothing to do with participants' belief in God. Perhaps it was just a coincidence, and people with more positive views of God also took better care of themselves or had more social support. Maybe believing that God is forgiving puts people in a better mood, inspiring them to live a healthier lifestyle or take their antiretroviral medication more reliably. So Ironson and her team used a sophisticated statistical technique called hierarchical linear modeling to test for these possibilities. The result was that participants' views of God continued to predict both viral load and immune functioning even beyond these external trappings of religion. Beyond whether people are religious, it seems that the specifics of their beliefs really do matter.

Some forms of faith appear to be more comforting and help people to be more resilient than others. This isn't to say that any beliefs are necessarily wrong or right; that's a discussion better left to theologians and religious leaders. But some beliefs may buffer the savage insults of trauma more than others. Michael would need every ounce of that kind of faith he could get.

———

With Exodus ten years behind them, in 1989 Michael Bussee and Gary Cooper were living an ordinary life together in Anaheim, California. This would change, however, one morning when Gary found a spot under his tongue. Michael immediately recognized thrush, one of the early signs of a strange new illness that was traumatizing the gay community. So many people were dying of AIDS that activists were now calling its effects a gay holocaust. Michael and Gary's lives were transformed from tranquil to chaotic as they began visiting doctors to search desperately for a treatment, trying to make the most of every day. Their life together lasted only four more years.

"We were on the way home from a camping trip along the Pacific Coast Highway. Gary was so frail. I looked, and he'd stopped breathing and had quietly passed. . . . Did I think this is God's punishment? That this was my retribution for giving into the dark side?" Michael pauses, hesitant to answer. "For a while, I did."

Gary's death became the first in a succession of losses for Michael. The AIDS epidemic had decimated the gay community, and like many others, Michael lost numerous friends and loved ones.

He thought of the lessons he had learned about God's wrath when he was younger. He couldn't shake the thought that perhaps God really did have it in for gay people. Maybe God was punishing him for his sins, for leaving Exodus, for giving in to his homosexual nature. Maybe this was the hell he had been warned about when he was a child. These thoughts plunged Michael into despair and depression.

Then, at a moment when things could scarcely get worse, he became the victim of an antigay hate crime. He was leaving a theater with a couple of friends in 2002 when a group of men shouting gay epithets jumped them. Believing they'd gotten away from the attack with only scrapes and bruises, Michael saw on his way home that he and one of his best friends had suffered multiple stab wounds. Michael survived; his friend, Jeffery, bled to death on the operating table.

A decade of violence, illness, death, and self-hate had finally reached its peak for Michael. At first the assault added to his belief that God was punishing him. But something about this newest tragedy was different. He found himself wondering if any god, even the stern deity of his childhood, could be this cruel. In that moment, something changed for him. In the face of everything he'd endured, he found it impossible to believe that God could operate this way.

Michael's faith shifted away from one "that only reinforces guilt and shame and depression," he remembers. "That kind of toxic faith—that bad things happen to you because you're being punished by God and good things happen to you because you're doing the right things—that kind of fundamentalism is just dangerous."

Michael didn't give up his belief in God, but he found that it had changed. "Yes, I was still Christian," he says with conviction, "but I had to ask myself, 'What is this religion I believe in?'" His faith was still intact, was in some ways as strong as it had ever been; but it was time for a reorientation of an altogether different kind.

———

The plane landed at Israel's Ben-Gurion Airport on a bright spring day in 1979. The church group, originating from Milwaukee, Wisconsin, boarded a tour bus and headed southeast along Route 1 to the city of Jerusalem. The weeklong guided tour walked the steps of Jesus along the Via Dolorosa within the walled Old City to the Church of the Holy Sepulcher. It stopped at Bethlehem's Church of the Nativity and the slopes of the Mount of Olives. Among biblical landmarks, the group sampled falafel and purchased souvenirs from the souks.

One morning, two members left the group and took their own trip to Yad Vashem, Israel's memorial to the victims of the Holocaust.

James Cameron and his wife, Virginia, had talked a lot about traveling the world together. He'd done so much traveling on his own: to schools in the Midwest and the South, to lecture halls across the East and West Coasts. Not many people had escaped being lynched, so people were fascinated by his story. He and Virginia met not long after he was released from prison, and when he told her his story, he worried that the fact that he was an ex-con would drive her away. She told him it didn't matter to her how he was in the past; it was who he was now that mattered. James figured that if Virginia could see him for who he was now, maybe he could forgive himself after all these years.

At Yad Vashem, James encountered another shameful past. In one exhibit, he and Virginia slipped into a cool, dark cavern lit with what seemed like a million candles, each flame representative of a child murdered by the Nazis. He realized at that moment that sixteen-year-old James Cameron and the millions of children who had died at the hands of the Germans were linked by a substance far stronger than the hemp fibers of a hangman's noose. In the Hall of Names, photos of the dead mounted the high walls, floating above their heads like apparitions. The testimony from survivors of Auschwitz-Birkenau and of ghetto-enforced segregation spoke to James in a surprising way. When he and Virginia stepped back out into the bright Middle Eastern sun, he told her, "We need something like this, to talk about what happened to black people."

"He opened the first version of America's Black Holocaust Museum in his basement," says Fran Kaplan. "He had fifty years of personal archives, literature, history, and artifacts down there dating back through the Jim Crow era. People traipsed through his house to see it. It was small, but there was nothing like it, certainly not in Milwaukee."

The museum's popularity grew, and James moved it to a slightly larger storefront in inner-city Milwaukee. While it was still a rather amateur offering, for James the museum was his small contribution to a part of the world where bad things had happened. Much to his surprise, that small contribution got big attention. It soon attracted a large donation, and James was able to buy and renovate a twelve-thousand-square-foot boxing gym. He now had the space to bring in traveling national exhibitions and even set up a screening area. The permanent exhibits included a simulation of a slave ship's cargo hold, a gallery of lynching photos, and videos of Milwaukee's two hundred days of open housing marches. "The museum struck a chord," says Kaplan. "People went back home and would send him their heirlooms to add to the collections. Someone sent James a Klan outfit he'd found in an attic. Another guy sent him a piece of the lynching rope that someone had cut up and sold as souvenirs from the Marion lynching."

Among these museum exhibits was James Cameron, who was at the museum every day, even into his eighties. He invited conversation and always answered questions.

"They'd want to know how he survived," says Reggie Jackson, one of the museum's first curators. "For those of us who believe in God, no explanation is necessary. For those of us who don't believe in God, no explanation is possible. He felt there was a reason he survived. That God had a mission for him. He was to give something back to the world. That's what the museum was all about. His mission was to teach people—we think they know these stories, but they really don't. We have the assumption we know this history. It's taught in a super-ficial way. In-depth information will give a stronger sense of how it worked and help people defeat discrimination."

It was a powerful message, witnessed by powerful people. Vice President Al Gore walked amid the museum's fifteen-foot reproduc-tion of a slave ship's cargo hold. Julian Bond and John Lewis admired the museum's depiction of life in an African village before enslave-ment. In 1998 the museum's attendance was growing—as was its reputation, not just locally but internationally. In 1998 a BBC docu-mentary crew came to James with an unusual request: they wanted to take him back to Marion, Indiana, the place where it all began. James agreed, and with his permission, the BBC arranged a special meeting with a man James had never met before. His name was William, and in 1930, three boys were involved in the robbery and murder of his brother, Claude Deeter.

James agreed to meet William Deeter at a church in Marion. When the moment arrived, James didn't know how to feel: remorseful for his part in the crime, full of trepidation about the memories Marion still held for him, or anger for all the things he had lost in this small town. William and James, no longer boys, understood how seemingly simple acts of indiscretion could transform lives, tossing people into the self-powered gears of history. While innocent of pulling the trigger, James felt deeply responsible for the part he had played in the events that unfolded that fateful night. But when the moment to confront the past arrived, James found he neither needed to ask for forgiveness nor even had the chance to. "William threw his arms around James, and they embraced," says Kaplan. "Then William asked James to pray with him."

———

"Trauma deals blows to people's meaning-making processes because it tears them away from the comfort of their meaning-making systems," writes psychologist and well-known advocate for culturally sensitive therapy, Laura Brown, in her book *Cultural Competence in Trauma Therapy*. "It teaches them, in the words of a prayer that Jews recite during their period of atonement each year, that they are 'of little merit,' in Hebrew 'ayn banu maasim.'"

At its best, Brown writes, religion offers its adherents methods to "ward off realities of meaninglessness and randomness, whether they worship at the shrine of Vishnu, pray to Allah, say Our Father or the Shema, keep kosher or a vegan diet, or practice celibacy. Through these and other rituals of being human, they generally find ways to make meaning of their lives in the face of that essential meaninglessness and inject a framework of order onto chaos."

But Michael Bussee had not been lucky enough to have this kind of faith. Instead, the religion of his youth had given him the message that God was judgmental and even wrathful, a message that turned trauma into bottomless suffering. But now this had changed. "I still believed I had to love God with all my heart, soul, and might, and that we should love our neighbor as we love ourselves, but the doctrine, theology, structure, hierarchy, and theological debates over sexual orientation weren't helpful," he says. "I had to believe now that the Bible was written by men inspired to write about God, and sometimes these writers got it wrong."

Just as Gail Ironson found in her study of HIV-positive patients, Brown writes in her book that some forms of religious belief may be more helpful in the aftermath of trauma than others. "Belief systems that separate the kindness of a divinity from experiences here on earth can be protective at times of trauma," Brown writes. "Religious beliefs that include a sense of personal connection with a nurturing, parental God can also be protective because many trauma survivors describe being comforted by prayer and the sense that God is listening to them even if their pain and suffering are not immediately relieved."

Michael's spiritual journey had led him to just such beliefs, and these beliefs reinvigorated his existence. At this point, religion changed from a fount of constant burden to a source of great peace. It also gave him a sense of direction he hadn't had in years. He resolved to set things right.

"Exodus had become even more dangerous since I left. It had become an antigay movement. I felt despicable for being silent for so long," Michael says. "I was still a man of faith, but to me, as I saw it now, we didn't have to get rid of our faith and our sexuality. We could embrace both. That was the message, not the junk psychology, junk science, and antigay politics Exodus was spreading. As a former leader, I never thought I'd ever become an advocate for ex-gay survivors, or become a leader in a small but growing group of ex-gay leaders." But as a supersurvivor, this was exactly what he would become.

He'd taken small steps in the past, before Gary's death in 1991. In their absence, the organization had become part of a network of hundreds of ministries in seventeen countries. Gary said they couldn't in good conscience be silent anymore. But Michael was hesitant. He felt they had too much to lose. Going public would place them in a vulnerable position at a time when Michael needed to focus on caring for Gary. But Gary was adamant, so Michael called an attorney and scheduled a small press conference to warn others about the dangers of sexual reorientation therapy. They received a mixed response. Some in the gay community, for instance, praised them for coming forward, whereas others claimed they had blood on their hands. For its part, Exodus took steps to distance itself from Michael and Gary, going so far as to downplay their roles as cofounders. Even though there was growing debate regarding the effectiveness of sexual reorientation therapy within the organization itself, Exodus continued to reject any suggestion that its practices were harmful or that it should close its doors. At the time, beaten down by the controversy, Michael had decided it wasn't worth it to assert himself again.

But now, on June 27, 2007, spurred on by his transformed spiritual convictions, he was resolved to undo the wrongs he had done.

"My name is Michael Bussee. I want to thank you for this opportunity to tell my story. Thirty years ago, I helped create Exodus International. Today, I am here to apologize," began an open letter to the survivors of Exodus. "Today, I am . . . a proud gay man. But thirty years ago, I was not so proud. In fact, I grew up hating my gay feelings. I endured name-calling, bullying and beatings. . . . I desperately wanted to be straight. But how? At about age 12, I began a personal quest to find the 'cure' for homosexuality. . . . [But today, I am] one of Exodus' most persistent critics—not because I want to 'deny hope.' On the contrary, I want to affirm that God loves every person—and that God's love does indeed change lives. It has certainly changed mine. It just didn't make me straight.

"I have found harmony between my sexuality and my spirituality," he continued. "I am hopeful that others can do the same."

Despite his activism, public sentiment condemning the program, and even growing debate within Exodus itself, the organization refused to close. So when Michael was invited to appear on television with Alan Chambers, the president of Exodus International, for the Oprah Winfrey Network series *Our America with Lisa Ling*, he came up with a plan.

At the time, he led online survivor groups for hundreds of people who were recovering from the ill effects of ex-gay therapy, many suffering from posttraumatic stress disorder and depression. Michael asked group members if they would accompany him to the taping. Face-to-face with Alan Chambers, Michael and the other survivors offered their stories. "We made him listen. At the end of the taping, everyone was in tears," says Michael. "The survivors were in tears, the crew was in tears. Even Alan's wife was in tears."

On June 18, 2013, a week before the interview aired on television, Exodus's board of directors released a surprising statement apologizing to the gay community for its role in passing undue judgment. The next day, during what would be Exodus International's last conference, Alan Chambers announced that the institution would be closing its doors forever.

"For quite some time we've been imprisoned in a worldview that's neither honoring toward our fellow human beings, nor biblical," said Chambers in his address. "From a Judeo-Christian perspective, gay, straight or otherwise, we're all prodigal sons and daughters. Exodus International is the prodigal's older brother, trying to impose its will on God's promises, and make judgments on who's worthy of His Kingdom. God is calling us to be the Father—to welcome everyone, to love unhindered."

In Michael's transformation—not from gay to straight, but from fearful to fearless—he has become a principal organizer in a small but growing group of ex-ex-gay leaders. Fifty-four years after the trip to the public library that led to a shocking realization of God's judgment that would haunt him for decades, he is now on the road to becoming free of self-hatred. His new mission is to help others along that same road.

James Cameron's invitation arrived in his mailbox in 2005. Since the late sixties, social activists all over the country had become familiar with him, the antidiscrimination writings he published, and his community organizing. Today, at the age of ninety-one, Dr. Cameron's voice was reedy, and his hair and mustache had long ago gone white. But his boyish gleam and full, round face suggested that he and his legacy might live forever.

James still did public speaking engagements, but he was getting too weak to travel. One of his last appearances was at the University of Wisconsin, where he was awarded an honorary doctorate for his contributions to the civil rights movement. For everyone who knew Dr. James Cameron, the honor came as no surprise. "It's amazing to me how many people's lives this man touched, people who didn't know him personally, the volunteers, the young people, the older people, blacks and whites," says Fran Kaplan, who is now the executive director of America's Black Holocaust Museum. In 2008 the museum moved all its archives online, allowing Kaplan to use online analytics to track exactly who was visiting the museum. A year after the archives went virtual, she logged visitors from 171 countries. The museum still exists, Kaplan explains, because prejudice and injustice still exist.

Forgiveness, as we will explore deeply in the next chapter, does not come easily. The United States' reluctance to pass civil rights reform was maddening to James. Over time, however, he came to appreciate the godliness of forgiveness. "He often preached 'Forgive but never forget,'" says Kaplan. "He meant that it is important to acknowledge the past, even if it is traumatic or painful, but it is urgent to forgive those responsible so that you can go on with life, so you can grow." Moreover, she suggests, he eventually developed the courage to forgive himself. In 1991, James sent a letter to the governor of Indiana, the Honorable B. Evan Bayh III, to ask for a pardon. "I ask for this pardon because I know that God has forgiven me for the role I played in the initiation of a crime that resulted in the loss of three human lives," read the letter. "When the devil's envy had destroyed man, God's mercy restored him." Six decades after that fateful day in 1930, James Cameron received that pardon. A week later, Marion, Indiana, presented him with a key to the city.

And then, in 2005, the U.S. Senate announced it was going to pass Resolution 39, which called for lawmakers to issue an apology for the country's failure to outlaw lynching. James was invited to be a guest of honor at the passage ceremony. "When we arrived to the hall of Congress," says James's son, Virgil, "Senator Ted Kennedy came down to dad on his knee. They talked as though they'd been friends for years. To me, he'd always just been dad. But the world knew him as something else. . . . Senators Dick Durbin and Barack Obama spent a lot of time with him. If dad had known he was talking to the man who'd be the first black president, he wouldn't have believed it."

After lunch, the Secret Service escorted James and the others into a wood-paneled room for a press conference with the senators who had cosponsored the resolution. Flanked by Mary Landrieu, George Allen, and John Kerry, James was handed a microphone and asked by the media what the passage of the resolution meant to him.

As he spoke, praising the resolution's passage while denouncing the failure of the government ever to pass an antilynching law, the press's cameras flashed and flickered all around him like a million candle flames.

8

Forgiving the Unforgivable

Without forgiveness there can be no future for a relationship
between individuals or within and between nations.
—DESMOND TUTU

South Asia's Kingdom of Bhutan is known as the last Shangri-La. This patchwork of nine-thousand-foot mountain peaks, rushing rivers and lush watersheds, forests of cedar and hemlock, rocky highlands, plains of savannah grasslands in the shadow of the Himalayas, and freshwater springs is home to roughly a million people. In 2006 a *BusinessWeek* global survey rated the kingdom among the happiest countries in Asia and the eighth-happiest on the planet.

In the southwest region, just miles from the border of India, is the tiny farming village of Relukha. Bhutan is characterized by hundreds of individual settlements populated by the Ngalongs in the northwest, the dominant Sharchops in the east, and Lhotshampas in the south. Relukha was part of a group of about a dozen Lhotshampa villages like it. Aaron Acharya's father, Devi, was their leader.

"I wasn't close to my father. I was in awe of him. He was a disciplinarian," says Aaron. Devi was a tough, resourceful man and the highly esteemed patriarch of his fellow villagers. Aaron could show no weakness in front of him. "I couldn't look him in the eye. He was quite respected, was always providing support to people who asked it of him. He spent very little time with us at home. But I always knew he cared about me." Once, when Aaron was eight, Devi took him to visit a village in the forested region of Gaylegphug, three days' journey from home. They were traveling by foot when they came to the yellow mud bank of the mighty Mau River. Devi hoisted Aaron onto his shoulders and waded across. "I think about that river when I think about my father," Aaron recalls. "I'm reminded how he cared for me even while I was fearful of him."

Two years later, when he was only twelve years old, Aaron traveled for five days to Samchi, on the way to boarding school. After walking for nearly two days, he got on three buses and eventually arrived in Khaling, where he would spend the next five years in secondary school. Aaron excelled academically. He learned English and two other languages. His knowledge of history and the sciences put him at the top of his class. He passed the countrywide exam his final year and scored the second-highest grade in all of Bhutan. Each year, he returned to Relukha for vacation having fallen more and more in love with learning. This put him a bit at odds with the predominant ethos of the village, largely the home of rice, corn, cardamom, and fruit farmers. His family, resourceful by nature, had for generations raised cattle and crops on this land. But Devi envisioned Aaron with a different future that only education could provide. In 1992, Aaron received a college scholarship from the government of Bhutan; with Devi's blessing and high hopes behind him, Aaron left for India to get a degree in civil engineering. Devi believed his son was going to be a different sort of resource to his people, learning to design public works and build roads, bridges, and flood protection systems.

The true significance of that resource was something the people of Relukha could not yet imagine.

Aaron is a smiley fellow with a short, square chin and neat dark hair. He wears frameless rectangular glasses that match his conservative and measured demeanor. He dresses in slacks and sweaters and carries himself with an air of properness. It's hard to imagine how he maintained this demeanor when the Bhutanese government began enacting discriminatory citizenship laws against his people in the name of maintaining the country's Tibetan Mahāyāna Buddhist character. While he was away at school in India, security forces arrived in Relukha to evict the population from their homes and seize their lands. Making these actions legal required the locals, including Devi, to sign a so-called voluntary migration form. But the soldiers didn't count on Devi's strength of spirit. He refused to sign. In response, officials launched an operation of harassment and arrests.

Aaron returned for a holiday and learned of his father's incarceration. "A war had begun in my absence," Aaron explains. "It wasn't a war you ran from, but a war you were forced into at gunpoint." Aaron was determined to get his father back. The local agent of the central government had turned a small post office five hours from the village into a makeshift prison, where Devi was now being held. Aaron demanded that officials let his father go. Instead, they incarcerated Aaron, too. For five days and nights Aaron heard the jailers thrashing Devi and three of his friends in a neighboring cell. "He shouted and cried out," Aaron says of his father. "They hung him upside down. They beat him. They wanted me to hear. They probably wanted him to know I could hear."

On the fifth day of Aaron's arrest, two officers brought Aaron and Devi into an office. There, a menacing officer walked around his desk, glaring first at Aaron and then at Devi. "You're a troublemaker," the officer said to Devi. "Sign, and you can both leave tonight. Don't sign, and I'll kill you." To show he meant it, the officer fondled the pistol he had strapped to himself.

Devi shook his head. The officer crossed the room and punched Aaron's father hard in his belly.

"Dad, just sign," Aaron said. "We'll come back one day and get everything back."

The officer turned and leveled his gaze at Aaron. "What did you say?" He pushed the barrel of his pistol against Aaron's temple.

Another officer put a pen in Devi's hand. Aaron watched his father sign the documents. The eviction papers gave Devi and his family twelve days to leave the country. Another twenty-three families faced the same edict. Aaron's family had land, three houses, cattle, and crops they were now forced to leave behind.

The ancestral families of Relukha would caravan for three days to a tiny camp near the border of India. From there, they would travel toward another series of camps set up in neighboring Nepal by the Nepali government and the United Nations High Commissioner for Refugees. These camps, Aaron knew, were dangerous and lawless places filled with disease, violence, and squalor. But there was no choice.

It was a silent journey, on foot, back to Relukha from the jail. In Bhutan, Aaron explains, men do not cry, so Aaron hid his rage and despair. Devi had been beaten so savagely that he couldn't walk straight. If Devi had permitted him, Aaron would have carried him home. But Devi was a proud man. He would walk on his own. These crimes, Aaron thought, were unforgiveable.

———

Trauma happens to most people. We expect it to happen to people living in troubled parts of the world: war-torn nations and poverty-stricken regions. We expect it to happen to people in risky careers: cops, firefighters, rescue workers, and soldiers. Though it might not surprise you that people such as Aaron and his family were targeted, as we allude to in chapter 1, trauma also happens to somewhere between 50 and 80 percent of people in the developed world at some point in their lives. In 1990, Harvard Medical School professor of health care policy Ronald Kessler, along with the U.S. government and a large team of investigators, undertook the first large-scale field study of mental health in the nation's history. As part of the study, called the National Comorbidity Survey, researchers interviewed a representative sample of almost six thousand Americans ranging in age from fifteen to fifty-four, asking them detailed questions about their exposure to traumatic events. According to the results, a whopping 61 percent of men and 51 percent of women had experienced a traumatic event sometime in their lives. And these numbers are lower than some estimates, because the researchers didn't count as traumas such things as severe medical illness or the loss of loved ones.

The really sad thing is that many of these traumas are man-made. As Aaron and the villagers of Relukha experienced, many traumas are the result of people's cruelty and inhumanity to one another. Although it's difficult, because of variance between regions, to estimate exactly what percentage of trauma worldwide is man-made, it's clear that it's large. In the National Comorbidity Survey, for instance, if you add up the percentages of traumas involving rape, molestation, physical attack, combat, threat with a weapon, neglect, or physical abuse, the total comes to 45 percent in men and 43 percent in women. The figure for natural disasters is only about a third of that.

To make matters worse, the very people we love and are close to are often the ones who perpetrate crimes and injustices against us. The U.S. Department of Justice reports that about one in six women in the United States is raped during her lifetime. Contrary to popular belief, most people know their rapists. According to the National Violence Against Women Survey, a study of eight thousand women across the United States published by the National Institute of Justice in 2000, only about 17 percent of adult female victims were raped by strangers. The rest were victimized by people they at the very least were acquainted with. But a shocking 62 percent were raped by someone they knew pretty well—a spouse or ex-spouse, current or former live-in partner, date, or boyfriend.

These forms of victimization, sometimes called interpersonal traumas, are the most traumatizing of all. In the late 1990s, the World

Health Organization launched its World Mental Health Surveys Initiative, an ongoing program to review mental health across the globe. In 2010, Dan Stein, chair of the Department of Psychiatry and Mental Health at the University of Cape Town, South Africa, and a team of colleagues used data from the initiative to find out what sorts of traumatic events were most associated with suicidal ideation, plans, and attempts. They read more than a hundred thousand interviews related to trauma in twenty-one countries, and topping the list was sexual and interpersonal violence.

Given these depressing statistics, it's tempting to become angry and resentful, to view other people as threats and little more. That's what some victims of interpersonal trauma do, of course. They may hold grudges, harbor lifelong resentment, and even seek retribution. Who could blame them? A long review of history reveals no shortage of violent examples—whether we're talking about the generations of Jews and Muslims in the Middle East or classic conflicts among Serbs and Croats, Protestant and Catholic Irish, or northern and southern Sudanese.

From a safe distance, it's easy to see that grudges aren't healthy on a societal scale. But what about on an individual level? Technically, psychologists refer to grudge-holding and revenge-seeking as unforgiveness. It seems obvious that unforgiveness is bad for mental health—it's highly unpleasant to harbor anger, hostility, and hurt for prolonged periods of time. But science also is beginning to show that unforgiveness also may contribute to poor physical health. Psychologists Charlotte Witvliet, Thomas Ludwig, and Kelly Vander Laan asked seventy-one students at Michigan's Hope College to call to mind a person in their lives who had mistreated or offended them. While fitted with instruments to monitor heart rate, blood pressure, and sympathetic nervous system activity, students imagined both what it would be like to forgive the transgressor and what it would be like to harbor a grudge. The results were simple and to the point. When imagining harboring unforgiveness, the participants felt stronger negative emotions and experienced higher heart rate, blood pressure, and sympathetic nervous system activity than when imagining offering forgiveness.

These results dovetail with the findings of a 2010 replication of the National Comorbidity Survey mentioned earlier. Among the many questions in this extensive survey, ten thousand U.S. residents were asked, "Would you say this is true or false? 'I've held grudges against people for years.'" Writing in the journal *Social Psychiatry and Psychiatric Epidemiology*, researchers Erick Messias, Anil Saini, Philip Sinato, and Stephen Welch from the Medical College of Georgia find that people who said they tended to hold grudges reported higher rates of heart disease and cardiac arrest, elevated blood pressure, stomach ulcers, arthritis, back problems, headaches, and chronic pain than those who didn't share this tendency. Though most scientists note that much more research is needed on the subject, it's possible that the physiological agitation experienced by the Hope College students may actually erode health over the long term.

Unforgiveness certainly appears to be unhealthy. But aren't some truly horrible things simply unforgiveable?

———

Growing up in the city of Kigali, Rwanda's capital, Clemantine Wamariya was an inquisitive little girl. In fact, her unending wonder at the world around her caused even her endlessly loving parents to want to put tape over her mouth. "I remember driving through the city and the whole way asking my mother, 'Who lives here? What about here?' My mother made up stories from one house to another. I wanted to know everything."

With a short nose, high cheekbones, and a slender physique, Clemantine at twenty-four is striking. The first thing people often notice is her distinctive wide-eyed smile. She wears her hair in dozens of long Rwandan braids tied behind her head. Her skin is the color of a dust storm. She speaks with a yearning cadence that infuses wonder and horror as she talks about the events that began in 1994, only shortly after that drive through the city with her mother.

She was six when the mass killings started in Kigali. "The first thing they do is rape the girls," Clemantine says, drawn back to the memory of the genocide.

Ethnic tensions were brimming in Rwanda when a government assassination sparked the start of Hutu-conducted mass killings of Tutsis and pro-peace sympathizers. Trying to protect her and her sixteen-year-old sister, Claire, their parents placed them in hiding at their grandparents' home. But Clemantine's grandparents couldn't protect the girls from the violence for long.

She remembers the beginning of the massacre in snippets. The house was cold. The darkness was impenetrable. The night ushered in the sounds of annihilation, howling, and bawling, from the street. "There was lots of noise and banging outside. There was singing— actual *singing*—from the mob coming down the avenue as they broke into the houses. I heard crying in the dark. From inside or outside, I'm not sure. Then screaming. I was in a corner, shaking near my grandmother's bedroom. Claire and I scrambled in the dark, trying to find places in the house to hide. We didn't know where to go."

The sisters crept through an airless hallway to the far side of the house. Claire stopped short of the kitchen and opened a tiny window. From there, the sisters escaped to the yard and slipped into the darkness of a field of banana trees. Then Clemantine had a sudden horrible thought. She turned back to the house, but Claire yanked her deeper into the forest, seemingly incapable of stopping to consider the family they'd left behind. Claire lifted her sister up the trunk of a tall tree and ordered her to climb. Up in the yawning branches, time atrophied. Clemantine imagined transforming herself into a boulder, an inanimate piece of earth whose elements were frozen in time, anonymous and impermeable. All around them, far below, deafening shrieks and cries split the darkness as roaming death squads slaughtered neighbors with laser-like exactitude, much as they did all over the capital city that night and throughout the country. "Far away, I could see fire and smoke rising above the trees and rooftops," Clemantine says. "I didn't know if my house was on fire, too. We waited for my grandparents to get out." She pauses to find her next words. "This will never make sense to me. Not ever. What we saw. So much death. What we ran from . . . If I think about it too much it will make me crazy. My grandparents never came out."

In the morning, Clemantine and Claire emerged from the trees. They walked roads clogged with people lying motionless in the gutters. Needing a place to store the dead, houses of worship were converted to storerooms, where bodies were piled floor to ceiling. Across the city, houses smoldered. Clemantine and Claire joined other displaced victims of the ongoing assaults and walked many days to a refugee camp in Burundi. "We'd found ourselves in a place neither of us had ever imagined, surrounded by thousands of others, all wounded, lost, screaming, crying, and hungry; all in shock; all in disbelief," Clemantine says. Together, she and Claire stood in a long line for a tent, blankets, and sacks for their belongings. She and her sister stayed in the camp for roughly a year, during which time the Hutu massacred an additional eight hundred thousand Tutsi.

"Most of us usually then want to get our own back, but an eye for an eye ends up with everyone blind, as Gandhi noted," Archbishop Desmond Tutu tells us from his home in South Africa. The Nobel Peace Prize recipient rose to worldwide prominence as a vocal opponent of apartheid and a defender of human rights not long before the government of Bhutan began its campaign of ethnic discrimination. Considered one of the world's foremost experts on political forgiveness, Archbishop Tutu had presided over the South African Truth and Reconciliation Commission, which determined whether to grant amnesty to those who had committed abuses during the apartheid era.

"No one has the right to tell someone who has suffered that he must forgive," Tutu continues. "No, we have to enter into the anguish of the one who has been made to suffer, to ameliorate and understand and sympathize with their suffering."

Tutu is giving voice to what many survivors and experts agree is true. There should never be an obligation to forgive. Victims do not *owe* their victimizer forgiveness. To forgive is something highly personal that people do when and if they are ready. It's not something that anyone can or should force anyone to do. To apply such force further wrongs the victim. However, science seems to show that for people who naturally come to the point where they are ready to move beyond unforgiveness, to forgive is generally a healthy decision for them. It helps them to move forward in their lives, and indeed may help them to become supersurvivors.

But Aaron Acharya of Bhutan had a lot of reasons for harboring unforgiveness, had experienced a lot of wrongs that nobody could make him forgive. His scholarship to study engineering in India, awarded by the very government that was now persecuting him, had been revoked. Instead of returning to finish his degree, he had settled into temporary shelter in a refugee camp in Nepal with thousands of other refugees from Bhutan, many from his own village. Aaron's family, unlike other refugees who were registered in the camps before him, was given no living supplies, no cooking oil, no firewood, no vegetables, and no kerosene. Despite the shame it brought upon them, they foraged for firewood in the deep jungle so they could cook the meager rations they collected from the UN. Their new home was an overpopulated mix of tiny dark shanties, dense expanses of bamboo huts without sanitation. Many there died of malnutrition. Over time, conditions deteriorated, ushering in scurvy, malaria, cholera, and measles.

Aaron's father, Devi, tried to remain a strong leader among his people in the camp. It was clear to Aaron, though, that Devi was a shell of the man he'd been before the torture. "I don't know if my father blames himself," Aaron says. "He always thought he was the provider, not only to our family but to our neighbors, too. In the village, people looked to him. His understanding of his family, his village, was lost, along with that intangible sense of responsibility you can measure only in kind acts. He lost his home and his self-worth. He was dehumanized."

"I spent a lot of time wondering what I would do if I saw these people who did this to him on the street, in another life or situation," Aaron recalls.

One night, he was offered that chance.

A group of men came to see Aaron in his hut claiming they had found one of the people responsible for the family's eviction from the village. "We have no doubt it's him," they said. "Let's teach him a lesson he won't soon forget!" Aaron and a few others who had been victims of this man's brutality arrived at his hut in the new camp. The man who lived in this hut was once a member of the District Planning Committee and had worked alongside Aaron's father. During the purge, Bhutanese security forces had recruited Lhotshampa foot soldiers. This so-called colleague of Devi's became a low-level official who played a role in evicting his fellow villagers. "I was so angry at him and his collaborators," Aaron says. "I couldn't get over it. I wasn't sure what I'd do when I saw him. I wanted to understand what drives human beings to do what they do. The beating, jailing, and starving. Was it anger? Was it hatred? Because of the actions of this man, we'd lost everything. Is this what you do when evil gets into you?"

The man was not home, just his wife and children. Aaron pushed the door open and he and the other men let themselves inside. The children were sitting at a table in the middle of the hut. Not just any table, Aaron realized, but a table that the children's father had appropriated, by force, when Aaron's family had just a day to live in the village.

"Could I forgive this man? Could I move on without confronting him in some way? I did not know."

———

Though Archbishop Tutu is resolute that no one should or even can be forced to forgive, he is quick to add: "We can only hope that the sufferer will realize that not forgiving affects them as a human being, and hope that they will see that nursing a grudge is bad for their health—it can give one stomach ulcers."

We know from the research that what Tutu has realized through hard-lived experience is right. "Forgiving," the archbishop says, "is good for our health."

One intriguing research finding is a link between forgiveness and lower levels of depression. Psychologist Loren Toussaint at Luther College in Iowa, along with his colleagues David Williams, Marc Musick, and Susan Everson-Rose, analyzed more than fourteen hundred telephone interviews across the United States. These interviews allowed the researchers to assess a number of sensitive psychological issues. Depending on how participants answered a handful of screening questions, the interviewers would be prompted to ask in-depth follow-up questions. For instance, they asked participants if they had recently lost interest in things they used to enjoy, such as work or hobbies. If someone answered yes, follow-up questions tested for major depressive disorder. In addition to questions about mental illness, interviewers asked about people's tendencies to forgive others and themselves. According to the results published in the journal *Personality and Mental Health*, people's answers to the forgiveness questions were among the best predictors of their probability of having depression. It's not surprising that people's tendency to forgive themselves for wrongdoings they've perpetrated against others is associated with a lower probability of encountering depression. Guilt and shame can be pretty depressing. More surprisingly, however, people who tended to forgive *others* for wronging them also appeared to enjoy lowered probability of depression. This can't be explained by appealing to decreased guilt or shame; after all, those who forgive are the wronged parties. So the question is: why?

"Without forgiveness there is no hope," Archbishop Tutu famously said. He was referring to South Africa immediately following the abolition of apartheid, when resisting the tendency to seek revenge upon white leaders who formerly perpetrated human rights violations against the black majority seemed to be the only way to keep the nation from tearing itself apart. But he's also pointing to something much more personal: forgiveness of others appears to fuel hope. Though research on the topic is still in its infancy, forgiveness may play a more important role in nurturing hope than anyone ever thought. Along with the findings already discussed, Toussaint and his colleagues found that hope may be the link between forgiveness and lowered risk of depression. They found that less willingness to forgive predicted greater hopelessness, which in turn predicted greater depression.

Toussaint's study isn't the only one linking forgiveness with hope. In fact, one of the world's foremost researchers on hope, University of Kansas psychologist C. R. Snyder helped to develop a prominent theory of forgiveness. Along with psychologist Laura Yamhure Thompson and a team of researchers, he created a psychological test to measure forgiveness, called the Heartland Forgiveness Scale. In a 2005 study appearing in the *Journal of Personality*, they report strong correlations between this test, hope, and depression. To Snyder, who passed away just a few months after publication of that article, the link between forgiveness and hope seemed simple. "Forgiveness is giving up the hope that the past could be any different," he was fond of saying. Forgiveness means breaking the psychological ties that bind you to the past, giving up the quest to change what has already happened. As discussed in chapter 2, sometimes giving up on impossible goals can free people to experience the true hope, the *grounded* hope, of changing the future. But what does that really look like for someone who has suffered like Clementine?

———

Life as a refugee was nearly unbearable for Clementine and her sister. Over the next six years, they relocated to the Democratic Republic of the Congo. When war erupted there, they fled to Tanzania, then to camps in Malawi, Mozambique, South Africa, and finally Zambia. The locations changed, but the same poverty, lawlessness, larceny, rape, and death followed them. Someday, Clementine told herself, the people responsible for all this would be brought to justice so this would never happen again; someday she would search the continent to find her displaced family. The more time that passed, however, the more unlikely that reality seemed to become.

Clementine shares these memories in language filled with metaphors and striking imagery. Rwanda during the massacre, for instance, was "noise and chaos." The camps were "places where the mind and body were imprisoned, where your brain reverses and becomes your stomach. All you know is hunger and worry." This is part of what makes her such an engaging person. She paints a beautiful picture of horror. But as you spend more time with her, a different picture emerges, one in which these perceptions, much like any defense, kept her moving and alive.

When Clementine was a child, her nanny told her a story about a lost little girl. But this girl was different from all other girls. Born of a thunder god and a mortal woman, when this girl smiled, glass beads fell from her lips. And so the lost little girl smiled through her fear, knowing that her mother would follow a glimmering trail to find her again. "I saw myself as this little lost girl in the story," Clementine explains. In the refugee camps, she wrote her name on walls to mark her way, in the hope that her parents might follow the trail back to their daughter. As she moved from country to country, she walked the streets looking at people's faces. "Maybe I'll see someone that looks like me, and know it's my parents."

In 2000 Clemantine and her sister worked with the International Organization for Migration to obtain refugee status in the United States. That summer, they boarded a plane from Zambia to Zurich, where the passengers looked clean and well-dressed. From Zurich she flew to Washington, DC, feeling more lost than ever. The last leg of their journey brought them to Chicago. "I was filled with mixed emotions," she says. "I was happy to leave the horror, but I worried I'd never see my mom and dad again. When I was traveling from camp to camp, I would count how many mountains I passed so I could find my way back home. In a plane, I couldn't leave any trace behind to let my parents know where I'd gone. They were lost. I was lost."

Her first host family had a fridge stocked with embarrassing amounts of food. "I'd open the refrigerator and just stare," she remembers. "I thought I was dreaming this luxury. There was a drawer of green apples there that I just kept on staring at. There were so many people I'd left behind that didn't have this food. How many months would we be able to make this one fridge last in Zambia?"

In 2001 there came two revelations. Clemantine's sister, Claire, had recently met a Rwandan businesswoman in Chicago, and together they'd made a nearly impossible connection. The woman had a friend back in Rwanda who, oddly enough, knew a friend of their aunt—an aunt whom they thought had been murdered. The woman made a call and got a phone number. That night, Clemantine sat in the corner of the living room and watched Claire dial. "It was silent for a long time," Clemantine says. "Then Claire started talking into the phone, and she smiled. I knew it was her. It was my aunt. She was alive. She thought Claire was lying about her identity. She thought we were dead." Then her aunt said something that turned Claire's face to stone.

Their parents were alive in Rwanda.

"It was like digging up the grave and watching them walk out," Clemantine says. "They were still invisible to me and so far away. In some ways, it was harder to know they were alive, because I couldn't get to them. We didn't know what to do. I wanted to reach through time and space and pull them back to me."

The second revelation came in the form of Elie Wiesel's memoir *Night*, from which Clemantine first learned the word *genocide*. Wiesel's survival in the Nazi concentration camps was revelatory to Clemantine. He was the first person to describe accurately the pain and confusion she herself had endured. Clemantine was so moved that she wrote an essay for a contest put on by *The Oprah Winfrey Show*, about the scar of genocide that marred both Germany and Rwanda. A few months later, she was shocked to learn that her essay was a finalist, earning her a seat at a taping of the program.

On the day of the taping, Clemantine put on a black pantsuit with wide lapels. She drove with her sister to Harpo Productions in the Near West Side of Chicago. The set was smaller than it looked on television.

Partway through the taping, Oprah did something, well . . . very Oprah. She invited Clemantine and her sister, Claire, to join her onstage. Oprah was holding an envelope. "This is from your family in Rwanda . . . and I wanted you to read it," Oprah said. Clemantine took the envelope and slipped her finger along the opening. But Oprah put her hand on Clemantine's and said, "You don't have to read it right now in front of all these people because"—Clemantine laughed nervously—"your family is here."

Clemantine's breath disappeared. Claire reached her arms out into the air to try to brace herself from falling. Behind the sisters a panel slid open. Their parents rushed out to embrace them. Unbeknownst to the sisters, *Oprah* producers had worked weeks to locate Clemantine's parents and had flown them back to their children.

"I fell on the floor," Clemantine recalls. "I raised my hands up and said, 'Thank you, God!' I squeezed my father and held my mother. No one had seen that private pain in me that I'd been carrying for twelve years since they were torn from us." The girl who smiled beads cried and mourned. "I let it go. The pain was gone. I could forgive," she says. "I could forgive. I could forgive."

———

Clemantine's journey toward forgiveness had begun years before her appearance on *Oprah,* though. Shortly after arriving in the United States, she'd picked up a strange new hobby. Every day, she collected the newspaper and saved the obituaries of strangers. She amassed hundreds of names, folding the pages and keeping them safely in her bedroom closet.

Clemantine now recognizes this as one symptom of a general obsession with memory. She was disturbed by the fact that what had happened to her, her family, and hundreds of thousands of others in Rwanda might not be remembered, honored, or mourned. In stark contrast, the names in the obituaries "were being recorded and honored," she says, her eyes pooling with tears. "They were not buried in unmarked holes in the dirt. Someone cared enough to write about the dead."

Clemantine believes that acknowledging and grieving her own trauma was an important step on her road to forgiveness. Forgiveness researchers tend to agree. A number of researchers have developed so-called "process models" of how people ultimately arrive at forgiveness. Though these models differ in their details and terminology, almost all of them observe that victims must pass through a stage of acknowledging the suffering that the wrongdoing has caused, admitting that it may have forever changed their lives, and owning their feelings of sorrow, loss, resentment, and sometimes rage.

Psychologist Robert Enright and psychiatrist Richard Fitzgibbons developed one of the most influential therapeutic approaches for helping people forgive. "This can be an emotionally painful time," they write in their book *Helping Clients Forgive.* "Yet, if the client or patient concludes that he or she is suffering emotionally because of another's injustice, this can serve as a motivator to change. The emotional pain can be a motivator to think about and to try to forgive." It was through this process, which Clemantine calls "mourning," that she realized she'd already lost enough valuable time and energy to the trauma, and decided she needed to find a way to move beyond the hurt.

A second commonality among most process models of forgiveness is the idea that it is useful to understand why the perpetrators did what they did, taking their perspective. "We ask a series of questions to challenge the person's view of the offender," write Enright and Fitzgibbons. "The point of all questions is to help the patient see a person who is, in fact, a human being and not evil incarnate." As distasteful as this may sound, this harkens back to an idea we began with: trauma often begets cycles of unforgiveness and revenge. Many perpetrators were once victims themselves. Understanding their pain may help victims move forward.

This is exactly what Clemantine naturally found herself doing. "I'm not just a girl who survived genocide and war," she explains. "I have learned to love others, even the people who did the killing. Before, I saw people as either friendly or dangerous. I now see that we are all bound by a universal desire to live. Every human being strives for this. They would kill each other to live. Who was my persecutor? I have no idea. They killed, but most murderers, they knew that killing is wrong. But there was a campaign of fear and misinformation everywhere.

"I can't be a part of that anymore," Clemantine continues. "That wouldn't have brought my parents back. Forgiveness allowed me to wash my burdened past away." She came to a simple yet freeing conclusion: she could not change the past. Rather than dwelling on the past, she found herself asking the hopeful and forward-looking question "What now?"

In the past, Clemantine was fighting for her life, but that past was unfixable. In the present, Clemantine was alive. As for the future,

Clemantine's life could now go in any number of directions. Where would it go next?

———

Aaron Acharya wondered something similar as he waited in a hut at a refugee camp for the return of the man who had betrayed his father and helped force the eviction of his village. How could he possibly forgive this betrayal? What purpose would forgiveness serve? Forgiveness wasn't going to save his people!

Aaron had every reason to want to spill this man's blood as a proxy for all those responsible for the expulsion.

The man came home that night to find Aaron and his friends ready to teach him a lesson. "I wondered what he was thinking when he did this to my village. Did he regret what he'd done?" asks Aaron. "We told him, 'We are angry. You are a horrible person.' And it was very strange because [he] admitted what he did. 'I made a horrible mistake. But look, they took away everything from me, too, and now I don't have anything anymore. You can do what you want to me. Just make sure my wife and kids will be okay.'" At that moment, Aaron took his enemy's perspective and understood what had happened.

"The foot soldiers in war, doing the prosecution, beating, jailing, and starving—these people don't generally get to make the decisions," Aaron says. "They are also doing what they do to stay alive. Nothing I could do to this man on this night would change what happened in Relukha. Here I am in his little hut in the camp, and I see his wife, who is dependent on him. I look at his children. They are hungry, naked, looking up to this father as a provider. I decided I would look after their father. If something were to happen to this man, what will happen to his children and wife? There is something deep inside each one of us that goes out to the underdog of the moment, no matter what that person has done before."

"To forgive is to abandon one's right to revenge," comments

Archbishop Tutu, reflecting on his own experience. "It is to give the other, the offender, the chance to make a new beginning. To forgive is to say, 'I refuse to be a victim.'" Whether or not this man who had betrayed Devi's village deserved to pay for what he had done, Aaron recognized that to exact revenge would be to continue the cycle of violence, to stoke the fires of anger, and to victimize others.

Aaron had gone to the hut, he says, to teach his neighbor a lesson. But teaching someone a lesson has multiple meanings. "I started out wanting to teach him a lesson through revenge, but left teaching him a lesson through education, how to reform. I probably taught myself a lesson that day, a lesson in forgiveness," Aarons says. "Over time we worked with him. We talked about what he had gone through in his life. He visited my father and me a lot after that. Our relationship eventually returned to normal. We patched things up. We taught him that there was potential in him to still do good."

But this process wasn't easy. Aaron was still plenty angry. It was virtually impossible for him to see anything but loss all around. "But I realized I had to forgive to push forward, otherwise I'd be lost in my anger," he says, and then pauses before making a persuasive distinction. "There's a difference, by the way, between forgiving and forgetting."

Though the science may show that forgiving is healthy, virtually all psychologists also make this important distinction, observing that forgetting is at best impossible and at worse unhealthy. As we've seen, remembering and expressing the pain of the wrongdoing seem to be important parts of the process of forgiving. But Aaron doesn't see forgetting as the least bit desirable. Tutu agrees. "Forgiving is not pretending you have not been wronged. This must be acknowledged," he asserts.

Aaron had seen far too much awfulness to forget. He would make certain that others remembered the injustices toward his disenfranchised people. Beginning in 1992, the United Nations Refugee Agency and other NGOs, at the request of the government of Nepal, started providing food, shelter, and nonfood assistance to the Bhutanese refugees. Aaron was the highest-educated person from his village and at the new camp his family had been transferred to, so he volunteered to document the human rights abuses of his people. Collecting these stories of torture and survival acted as a sort of catharsis—the kind of acknowledgment and expression of feelings observed in many process models of forgiveness. In the beginning of his documenting, he wanted to promise justice to every victim of torture. But he realized that this was an impossible goal. Over time, he began to train his focus on the future more than the past. The United Nations High Commission and the German embassy arranged for him and many others like him to receive a college scholarship. There was still a chance at reclaiming his old life. The scholarship didn't cover the high cost of an engineering degree, but Aaron had a different plan now. The refugee camps needed journalists. As a reporter, he could bring the refugees' stories to the world.

In 1998 he graduated from the University of North Bengal, in Darjeeling, India, with a degree in English literature—the closest thing the university offered to a journalism degree. He continued to be involved in Bhutanese human rights organizations and traveled throughout India for the Youth Organization of Bhutan, raising awareness and support for the Bhutanese refugees.

"I saw a need to speak about what I'd seen to whoever would listen," Aaron says. "The world needed to hear that my story was typical of the one hundred thousand refugees who required help to restart their lives." He had given up the false hope that he could somehow correct the past. Now it was time to make the future better, and for as many people as possible.

In late 1999, Aaron arrived in San Francisco to attend a conference on behalf of a Bhutanese refugee organization. He wanted to stay and raise awareness about the Bhutanese refugee crisis. So he applied for asylum. With the support of organizations such as Global

Youth Connect, he relayed the plight of his people to anyone who would listen. He waited tables, slept in strangers' living rooms. He thought about what had happened that fateful year back in Relukha. But he had to move on. In 2013 he transferred to Manhattan for a job working for the survivors of torture like his father. There, continents removed from the turmoil of Bhutan, he believed there was an opportunity to promote change. He managed the Human Rights Clinic for the global health organization HealthRight International, then known as Doctors of the World USA. He oversaw the forensic evaluations, affidavits, and testimony of more than three thousand torture survivors seeking asylum in the United States. Invigorated by this work, he steeped himself in the nuances of asylum law and immigration court practices. Within a year of immigrating to America, he became an expert on human rights violations and developments in the field of torture treatment. He also raised grant money for the program.

Due to the hard work of many international organizations, leaders in the refugee camps in Nepal, and activists such as Aaron, an opportunity arose to resettle Bhutanese refugees in the United States. Enthusiastic, Aaron visited the refugee camps in Nepal soon after this decision.

It was during this visit that he was met with some surprising opposition. "There was an uproar in the refugee camps when I came back," he says. "Many people wanted to come to the U.S., but they wanted justice more. For them, justice was returning to their homes." While Aaron didn't agree, he understood; he'd held that view once himself. Hoping to return to how things once were, his father remained in the refugee camps and refused to leave for these same reasons.

Eventually, however, people relented. They started arriving in the United States in large numbers. Their arrival sparked a new great need. "For the uninitiated, the U.S. is a very strange and unnerving country," Aaron says. "Refugees don't know how to immediately fend for themselves. They come here without legal representation, with no understanding of the laws, no access to medical care, and without any resources or finances. When they get here, they are really quite alone." Using his knowledge of the law, immigration courts, asylum offices, mental health providers, medical clinics, and resources, Aaron had a big new goal.

The idea was to establish a charitable cultural, social, and advocacy program for the needs of the Bhutanese people in the United States. In 2007 he and a number of his friends founded the Association of Bhutanese in America. The organization hoped to become the portal to a new life for thousands of Bhutanese American families, providing counseling services, job networking opportunities, and other resources to help the refugees integrate into American society. "If old ladies can tailor," Aaron says, "we would get them needle and thread."

Today, the organization is a resource specifically for Bhutanese exiles in the United States. It also serves a unique role as America's largest carrier of Bhutanese cultural identity, with programs to maintain ties to a country that betrayed its refugees, a country they once called home and might someday forgive.

————

As for Clemantine, she and her sister survived six years in seven refugee camps, witnessed the unspeakable, and found their long-lost family with the help of arguably the most powerful woman in the history of American show business. Although there was more than a bit of luck involved, Clemantine is also sure she made it happen herself. "I felt strength to take steps out into the world for the first time," she says. "I would no longer be a victim. I wasn't going to take what life gave me. I was going to go after things." We've called this broad belief in one's ability to go after goals grounded hope, and it's what led Clemantine to send her essay to *The Oprah Winfrey Show*.

Marshal Goldsmith, from chapter 3, called it trying many different things. Clemantine calls it growing into knowledge.

During her junior year at Yale University studying comparative literature, Clemantine joined Oprah to travel to South Africa to speak at the Oprah Winfrey Leadership Academy for Girls. In a letter home to friends, Clemantine later wrote, "I am not as afraid of the future as I used to be because some places, like that school, are creating leaders who listen. I cannot wait to see [the students] in action once they have built a strong intellectual foundation. My journey here has left me hopeful and inspired."

Clemantine writes that forgiveness is a journey—and not necessarily one she has fully completed. That journey, however, continues to teach her how to be a whole person again. Today, she brings this message to people all over the world. When she lectures before audiences at the United Nations, the U.S. Department of Homeland Security, human rights law conferences, and high school assemblies, they don't hear a story of vengeance. "It's a story about hope," she says with a smile that could only come from wisdom.

On October 28, 2011, President Barack Obama appointed Clemantine to a key post as a member of the United States Holocaust Memorial Council, alongside her hero Elie Wiesel. "These fine public servants both bring a depth of experience and tremendous dedication to their new roles. Our nation will be well-served," the president announced.

Yet no accomplishment, title, or feat of supersurvival has made the past fade from Clemantine's memory. On quiet nights in her dorm room, she still thinks about the screaming in the forest. But she is not bound to that past. She has found ways to channel that tragedy into great accomplishments, hopeful forays into a future she is determined will be better. Besides accumulating obituaries, Clemantine collects vintage buttons. Buttons are remarkably simple and beautiful objects of metals, glass, pearl, and bead. More than just fashion trimmings, they serve the specialized purpose of fastening and keeping things together. Today, when bad memories come flooding back, Clemantine calms her mind in the act of sewing the buttons into bracelets of tight piles on six-inch strips of heavy fabric. She wears these button bracelets on her arms. "Can you see the anger behind the bracelets when you look at them? See, I've transformed the anger into something beautiful," she says.

The girl who smiled beads now wears them on her wrist.

9

The Right Choice

There is scarcely any passion without struggle.
—ALBERT CAMUS, *THE MYTH OF SISYPHUS*
AND OTHER ESSAYS

Of the seven thousand people in attendance at Los Angeles's Staples Center, and the twenty-nine million television viewers, it was rock violinist Asha Mevlana, the supersurvivor we met in chapter 1, who had the best vantage point from which to watch the *American Idol* finale.

The *Idol* band ripped through theatrical performances with Queen Latifah, Jason Mraz, Keith Urban, Fergie, and other surprise guest stars. A vital onstage player in this iconic company, Asha was vibrant, her high cheekbones elevating what would ordinarily have been a bright smile into something radiant. A dark scroll of hair dropped over her right shoulder as she led into the opening notes of "Smooth" and Carlos Santana entered from stage left. Amid bombastic pyrotechnics, KISS descended from a giant hydraulic platform to the legendary modulations of "Detroit Rock City." Later, Queen joined the band for the night's penultimate performance, "We Are the Champions."

In 2008, Asha was hired for the position of electric violinist in the string section of the *American Idol* band. For the past two seasons, she had helped supply the show's live sound track, performing on national television. It was still hard to fully grasp that, roughly three years earlier, she was a public relations manager at a Manhattan start-up, with far different plans for her life. "I had a five-, ten-, and fifteen-year plan. I was going to go onto senior management, have kids, buy a couple of houses, and maybe own my own business. Something in public relations or marketing, I'm sure," she says, trying hard to remember what her life was like before she was told it might end far too soon.

Ricky Minor, the band's leader, signaled thirty seconds until they were back live. Asha took a sip of water from her bottle, tucked it back on a table offstage, and picked up the bow of her instrument. She walked with host Ryan Seacrest back onto the stage and took her position with the band, directly behind the final two contestants. The theater lights dimmed from jasmine to red. Seacrest was handed the results in a sealed envelope. "After a nationwide vote of nearly a hundred million, the winner . . . of *American Idol* . . . 2009 is . . ." Seacrest was playing with the audience as one might pluck a string, manipulating its tension. He was, after all, concealing in his hands an announcement that would forever change the lives of two hopefuls, for better or for worse. The moment he pronounced the winner, an exhilarating blast of light swallowed the stage and a tempest of confetti rained from above, covering Asha and the rest of the *Idol* band as they powered into a victory tune. She drove her bow across her violin, her final performance full of heart and bravura.

While Kris Allen walked away the season's victor, Asha couldn't help but feel that she, too, had won a game, one she'd started more than a decade before. Only, unlike the results on *America Idol*, her news hadn't come in an envelope, but in a most unlikely form—an ultrasound that announced her breast cancer. She caught it early and underwent a lumpectomy, chemotherapy, radiation, and hormone treatments. But the onslaught that would eventually make her a supersurvivor didn't stop there.

Given her family's cancer history, in combination with the fact that her breast cancer was estrogen-receptor positive, Asha's doctors told her she may be at a heightened risk of developing later ovarian cancer. To save her, they recommended a precautionary oophorectomy, a surgery to remove her ovaries and eradicate the danger altogether. Although this operation might save her life, it would eliminate her ability to have children. But Asha felt strongly that she wanted a family someday. So she sought a second opinion, and then a third. Unlike the *American Idol* judges, her doctors were unanimous.

Fortunately, the risk of developing ovarian cancer was statistically minimal until the age of thirty-five. This gave Asha more than a decade to put off the procedure, plenty of time to meet someone and have children. But having children wasn't what was most on her mind at the conclusion of her cancer treatment. After those initial moments of shock and terror, she also felt an unmistakable, unexpected impulse to live life as if there were no tomorrow. "I didn't know if I had five months or five years," she says. "I took a look at my life and asked myself what I really wanted to do with the time that I had."

Becoming a rock star was not part of any five-, ten-, or fifteen-year plan. Before suffering through her treatment, Asha enjoyed playing the violin, but she never considered leaving the security of a corporate job for the financially uncertain life of a struggling artist. Nor had she contemplated moving to California, thousands of miles from the social support that had gotten her through the darkest moments of her illness. When she told her friends she was leaving for L.A. to scratch out a living as a professional musician, they quite reasonably started to worry for her. Most of them didn't even know that the twenty-eight-year-old played the violin, let alone harbored any desire to go pro.

Judging by her performance, as Asha played season eight of *American Idol* into the credits, and the archives of television history, she saw clearly that her risky choices had paid off. At the same time, she would be the first to admit that stories like hers were rare, even for supersurvivors.

So how was it that Asha so quickly, and improbably, reshaped, reformed, and rerouted the path of her life?

Asha's story reflects many of the principles we've talked about in this book. Her confrontation with cancer forced her to reflect deeply on her fragile mortality. She could no longer tell herself that life would go on indefinitely, and she began questioning the choices she had made automatically up until her diagnosis. The shock shattered a worldview that previously told her that life was safe, predictable. Her unquestioned ten-year plan no longer comforted her. And she couldn't reassure herself with simplistic positive thoughts that everything would work out fine. That's what she *used* to think, but not now.

So she mustered the courage to stare the reality of her cancer, and the uncertainty of life, directly in the face and ask herself, "What now?" She set a new, lofty goal to become a professional musician, and took steps to learn and hone her craft, making calculated decisions that brought her closer to achieving this goal. Her small early successes created the building blocks of self-confidence, the slight positive illusions of control she needed in order to believe she had a chance of playing with Dee Snider and Mary J. Blige. She started on a path of grounded hope. All the while, she widened her net of social support, reaching out to newfound friends in the music industry. They encouraged her to follow her passion, so that when big things started happening for her, she felt the support she needed to see just how far she could go.

All this may make Asha's journey sound straightforward. But supersurvival is rarely easy.

———

From the stories in this book, some may conclude that supersurvivors have it good. After all, we've profiled Hollywood stuntmen, world-record holders, successful businesspeople, and human rights activists who have helped change the world. The natural human tendency is to place people with such accomplishments up on a pedestal and conclude that they're not like the rest of us. Nearly all the supersurvivors we've spoken to have been called special, gifted, or even heroes. And nearly all of them reject that label.

This is part of what led Maarten van der Weijden, the leukemia survivor who won the Olympic gold in swimming, famously to tell a newspaper reporter to stop comparing him with Lance Armstrong. But Maarten isn't alone in this sentiment. Casey Pieretti might have become a highly sought-after stunt person after losing his leg to a drunk driver, but he's also quick to point out that his livelihood is dependent on his phone ringing, just like everybody else's. And as far as his journey from survivor to supersurvivor is concerned: "I felt from the moment of the accident I wanted to live. There's nothing remarkable about that." Paul Watkins's decision to give up millions of dollars to become a priest after the shocking death of his friend, the copilot of American Airlines Flight 77, may seem remarkable to outsiders, but Paul says he was just pursuing another interest. "Yeah, I gave [my company] up," he says, laughing. "But it wasn't *that* great. I had millions in the bank, a lot on paper in stock. I just thought I was ready for a change."

When survivors experience amazing recoveries, we are often quick to label them inspirations—and not just in an "it's amazing you survived" kind of way. Many of us are quick to assume that these people are amazing and inspirational in all other ways as well. In short, we assume they must be special people.

Psychologists have a term for this: the halo effect, a phenomenon first documented by the great psychology researcher Edward Thorndike in 1920. The halo effect is a kind of cognitive bias in which our evaluation of someone's character is unduly influenced by our overall impression of him or her. Most research on the topic concerns physical appearance and has shown that the halo effect really matters. For instance, some studies have shown that jurors are more likely to assign more lenient sentences to attractive people than to less attractive ones.

Because people are beautiful or handsome, if we're not careful, we may assume they're also good people deep down.

We seem to do something similar for survivors. Because someone's survival story is inspirational, we jump to the unwarranted conclusion that he or she, as a person, must also be inspirational, even in ways we haven't directly observed. We're not saying that supersurvivors don't deserve credit for what they've accomplished; they clearly do. We're also not saying that their stories and the principles they exemplify shouldn't inspire us; they should. But if we are to learn from their trials and triumphs, it's important that we not make them into something they're not.

The supersurvivors we've interviewed often insist that they're ordinary people trying to make their way in the world. They see themselves as doing what anyone else would have done in their situations: making the best choices possible given what life has thrown at them. To them, it was their choices that helped them to rise up after trauma and claim the future they wanted for themselves. And of course, choices aren't always easy, any more than supersurvival is.

———

After the *American Idol* season ended, Asha chose to return to Porcelain, a rock band she'd joined shortly after moving to Los Angeles in 2007. The lone American in the five-person Australian group, Asha, along with her bright purple violin, was a unique addition to the usual clutch of guitarists, bassists, drummer, and vocalists. Porcelain's exigent mash-up of big vocals, ambient underpinnings, and power pop thrusts led to sold-out venues and a recording deal with Universal Records. Porcelain produced a debut album. The band's first single was getting heavy play on MTV Europe and on Australian pop radio, so now the label sent Porcelain on an Australian tour.

The three-month stretch was a blur of cities, hotels, radio station stopovers, bars, and rock venues from Sydney to Melbourne, Victoria,

Perth, and Wollongong—so many locations that Asha couldn't tell them apart anymore. The response to Porcelain's music was so strong that the label kept extending the tour. This was fine by Asha; she could picture herself staying in Australia forever. Why not? She hadn't followed a traditional life path. There was no reason to start now. Her life had ceased to follow a practical trajectory when she developed cancer and chose to radically change things for herself. She had been happy with this choice.

But in the time it had taken her to finish cancer treatment, earn a chair in the *America Idol* band, and witness the rise of her own band, eleven years had passed. She was now thirty-three years old, and despite her indisputable beauty, talent, and success, she was still single and without children. With the age-thirty-five deadline fast approaching, she had little more than a year to get pregnant before the operation to remove her ovaries would be necessary. But the Los Angeles dating scene was a challenge, and touring made romance that much more difficult. "Let's say I met someone," she says. "Two weeks later I'd be back on the road. That's no way to sustain a relationship."

There were other methods of having children, of course. She might freeze her eggs and opt for in-vitro fertilization or undergo intrauterine insemination. But these options typically involve hormone injections, and Asha's cancer had been hormone receptive. So her doctors recommended extreme caution.

Time had gotten away from her. Asha wondered about the odds of winning this game, the cost of losing it, and the wisdom of all the choices she'd made to reach this supposedly wondrous height.

———

Life presents a constant stream of choices. Some of these choices are big—what to study in school, whom to marry, or where to live. Most of them are small—which brand of toilet paper to purchase or which store to buy it from. Regardless of the kinds of choices we consider, the sheer number of options available to most people has increased dramatically in the past century.

A recent visit to a local grocer's breakfast cereal aisle revealed a staggering array of 220 options, with twenty-two granola cereals alone. The cheese section is even more daunting, presenting the consumer with 391 varieties. Buying a package of parmesan cheese becomes an ordeal: block, shredded, shaved, powdered; in a tub, shaker, or bag; fresh refrigerated or dry; mixed with other varieties of cheese. What exactly are the three types of cheese in the Italian Blend? And do all the different bags labeled "Italian Blend" contain the same mix?

All this may sound prosaic, but life presents us with more serious choices as well. People are increasingly given the message that they can choose to be anyone they want. In her book *The Tyranny of Choice*, philosopher Renata Salecl explores the downside of, as she calls it, "the dominant ideology of the developed world: the individual is the ultimate master of his or her life, free to determine every detail." Salecl isn't denying that choice can be good. Though there's still much progress to be made, it's good that more people in the early twenty-first century than at any other time in history enjoy the freedom and means to pursue education and choose the career path that is right for them. It's good that, in most developed countries, people's choices about where to live, whom to love, and what kind of life to pursue are limited less than ever before by prejudice and discrimination. It's good that medical technology has evolved to the point where women like Asha have choices about how to address serious illnesses. As Swarthmore College psychologist Barry Schwartz wrote in a 2000 article in *American Psychologist*, "I think it is only a slight exaggeration to say that for the first time in human history, in the contemporary United States large numbers of people can live exactly the kind of lives they want, unconstrained by material, economic, or cultural limitations."

Being free to choose is wonderful. But Schwartz makes an additional intriguing observation: The unprecedented prosperity experienced by many and the overabundance of choices that prosperity affords would lead "one to expect clinical depression in the United States to be going the way of polio. Instead, what we find is an explosive *growth* in the number of people with depression . . . Some estimates are that depression is ten times more likely to afflict someone now than at the turn of the century. Thus, we have a puzzle."

In addition to being profoundly good, choice can be intimidating, and having so many choices can be profoundly terrifying. Freedom rightly means that nobody can tell us how to live our lives. We are ultimately responsible for our choices and, by the same token, for our failures. We're offered both the possibility of making the right decision and the risk of making the wrong one. The only problem is we don't have a crystal ball. We can't know until after we've committed to an action whether we chose correctly. That's what the great philosopher Jean-Paul Sartre meant when he wrote, "Man is condemned to be free."

This is an argument that existential philosophers such as Sartre, along with Søren Kierkegaard, Friedrich Nietzsche, and many others, have been making in various forms for nearly two centuries. Peter Lawler, Berry College professor and conservative blogger, sums up the core of their argument well: "Hell is the experience of 'pure possibility.' It's the experience of not knowing who you are or what you're supposed to do. It's to have no order or direction to your life except what you might quite arbitrarily choose for yourself. If you might be everyone or might do anything, you don't have what it takes to turn your life in any 'particular direction.'"

Recently this classic perspective has received a flurry of scientific support. Sheena Iyengar of Columbia University's School of Business has produced a number of studies in the past decade that have changed the way psychologists think about choice. She has shown that the basic dilemma of choice is made even worse as the number of options at our disposal increases. In one study, appearing in the *Journal of Public Economics*, Iyengar and University of Chicago researcher Emir Kamenica tracked the contributions of more than

50,000 employees in 638 institutions to their voluntary 401(k) retirement accounts. Given the fragility of the United States' Social Security pension system, most financial advisers strongly urge their clients to contribute regularly and substantially to such accounts. One of the features of 401(k) accounts is the ability of employees to choose among a variety of funds in which to invest. But the number of fund options offered to employees can differ widely, ranging from only a few to fifty, sixty, or more. Happily, the researchers found that on average only 10.53 percent of employees didn't contribute anything to their retirement accounts. The astounding finding, however, was that this probability increases by 2.87 percentage points, or 27 percent, for every ten additional funds the employees could choose from. In other words, more choice leads to a greater tendency to choose nothing at all. This phenomenon, called decision paralysis, is one ironic downside to the surplus of choices we increasingly enjoy.

Such paralysis tends to occur when we are faced with either a very large number of choices—think fifty mutual funds or two hundred and twenty breakfast cereals—or a smaller number of equally attractive but different choices. The late Stanford psychologist Amos Tversky, who helped revolutionize the scientific understanding of decision making, and his colleague Princeton psychologist Eldar Shafir showed the latter in an experiment appearing in the journal *Psychological Science* in 1992. They asked college students to imagine that they were in the market for a CD player but hadn't decided which model to buy yet. As they were passing a store one day, they noticed a popular Sony model on sale for only ninety-nine dollars, a fantastic price. But it had to be purchased that day, because the sale would be over the next day and all the CD players would probably be gone by then. Not surprisingly, two thirds of the students said they'd buy the player then and there. Only the remaining third said they'd defer their decision until later. This makes sense; it's rational not to pass up a great opportunity. The interesting results came from a slightly different version of this question the researchers asked a second set of students. The students were told they were passing by the same store and saw the same popular Sony player on sale for $99. But they also saw that a top-of-the-line AIWA player was on sale for only $159, an equally deep discount over its usual price. Interestingly, under these conditions, almost half the students said they'd defer their decision. This wasn't because there was a dizzying array of choices, but because the two choices in front of them, though different from one another in some respects, appeared equally good. Under these circumstances, people tend to become paralyzed.

Life often confronts us with situations like those in these studies. On the one hand, we often face almost limitless possibilities, only to discover we can't possibly get enough information to make a reasonable choice. On the other hand, like Asha, we also often come to stark forks in the road. Have children or go all in with our career? Go back to school or stay in a steady yet unsatisfying job? Take a risk and move or stay where we are? Although the same psychological principles are probably at play, decision paralysis under these circumstances can lead to serious consequences. Asha felt the pressure, grappled with the indecision, and initially decided to kick the can down the road. She put off her decision to undergo a surgery that could possibly save her life but that would eliminate her ability to have children. But she also put off having children. Unlike Asha, not everyone in Tversky's experiment, or in life, becomes paralyzed. How do they avoid this fate? A man named Iram Leon may have the answer.

———

Even with a flat stroller tire, Iram was not going to give up. As he stood at the starting line, the Texas sunlight blinked in and out through the branches of the high oaks as heat lifted from the black pavement. The humidity was already seeping into his bones. The last time Iram ran a marathon, he threw up all over the course. Sometimes this happens when he takes his antiseizure medications. He wasn't trying to prove anything by running the Gusher Marathon in Beaumont today, except maybe to redeem himself from his last dismal run and beat his own best time.

Sitting in the stroller, Iram's daughter, Kiana, was six years old, a bright and happy kid with lots of friends. She loved to draw, so Iram had painted a chalkboard wall in her bedroom and pinned her pencil drawings up all over the house. He had been working in the garage recently when Kiana said, "Look what I made." She'd carved "I Love Daddy" in the wall with one of Iram's game darts. He'd framed that image in his mind, and thought of it while he ran, when the lengths of road grew too long and his body hurt. Then he started bringing Kiana on his runs, in a stroller, and then the hurt wasn't so bad.

Iram had arrived at the starting line in Beaumont, Texas, eighty-five miles northeast of Houston, only to discover that his stroller had a flat tire. He borrowed a friend's air pump, bent down to refill the tube, and the pump's lever broke off. Someone from his running team offered to watch his six-year-old so he could still compete, but the whole point was to spend time with her. Iram wasn't going without his daughter.

He looked around desperately for a solution and noticed someone in the crowd with a similar stroller. Iram negotiated a trade. They exchanged front wheels. He was buckling Kiana in when he realized the race was starting in two minutes. He took off jogging, panicked, weaving the stroller carrying Kiana through the mass of marathoners taking their starting positions. With seconds to go, Iram positioned himself with the stroller near a curb, to stay out of people's way, but he managed to frustrate two runners directly behind him anyway. If he was the only one dumb enough to race with a stroller and offset his time, no one was going to stop him, but he didn't have to block anyone else.

"Are they mad at us, Daddy?" Kiana asked.

"We're not going to block them," he said. "We'll let them pass." Marathon organizers and participants tended to frown on Iram running with a child in a stroller, worried the contraption would get in the way of other competitors. To accommodate everyone, Iram made a point of standing off to the side at the start of these races, out of the way of other, faster runners.

The starting whistle blew. As the race began, Iram realized that in his haste, he'd left both his shoes untied.

The marathon was moving around him. He leaned forward over the top of the stroller and said to Kiana, "We're off!" The next time he looked down at her, she was asleep.

Iram had been a runner his whole life. He was born in the city of Chihuahua, Mexico, and came with his parents to the United States in 1988. He first joined a track team in the third grade. He ran the 600-meter long-distance race. In high school he ran the mile and cross-country. On his thirtieth birthday he entered his first marathon and placed at about five hundredth, but he was determined to do better the next time. He continued training, and his time got better with each race. Much of this success is due to Iram's naturally competitive nature. Besides, he told himself, no one on his deathbed ever says I wish I'd gotten more sleep.

Running is a merit-based sport. Winning comes from training hard to build endurance and capitalize on natural athletic abilities. Iram's competitive personality pushed him toward excellence, a fact that served him well in almost every domain of his life. His goal in racing was to beat the others; outside running, his goal was the same. He beat every student in high school to become the class valedictorian. Then he graduated summa cum laude in four years from Pacific Union College with two degrees, in psychology and religion. In 2004 he was living in Austin and working for Travis County probation services, where for seven years he had excelled as an accomplished court officer. Running was not a metaphor for life; running *was* life, and the spirit with which he excelled on the track to reach elite times was the very thing that guided everything else in his life. His dream had always been to be the best, period.

Once, a friend asked him why he had never run one of those Races for the Cure. No one close to Iram had ever had cancer, so he'd never really given it much thought. A couple of days later, when Iram woke up unexpectedly in an ambulance, disoriented, his thoughts returned to the odd timing of his friend's question. He was in the ambulance because he'd experienced a grand mal seizure. At the hospital, he was tested for stroke, low blood sugar, and epilepsy. Later, he waited for the results of his brain scan. It revealed a tumor in his left temporal lobe. A later operation removed most of the mass, but the vestiges were beyond the reach of surgeons. Most tumors such as Iram's are fatal. The Duke University Hospital neurosurgeons who operated on Iram's brain told him the mean survival rate with treatment was about seven years. Age thirty at diagnosis, Iram found that the odds were he was not going to live past forty.

His daughter, Kiana, visited him in the hospital. She sat on his lap while he lay in bed, and he showed her the brain scan. She looked at the two-tone image with disappointment. "I thought I was gonna really see your brain."

"Just pictures, I'm afraid." He handed her the film, and her face brightened.

Iram and his wife were separating. In court, she brought up concerns that leaving Kiana in Iram's custody might be dangerous. What if he had another catastrophic seizure? His memory was becoming unreliable. He tried to hide his condition from his employer and colleagues, but his thinking was growing murkier. At work, he was making too many mistakes on the stand. Because he was unable to remember important facts, the county let him go.

"No matter what the doctors say, you'll be okay," Kiana said to her father. Iram put up a strong front, but really, he wasn't so sure he would be okay. He stopped running; he was a mess. His running team was trying to encourage him to come back to the sport; he refused. So soon after his surgery, Iram was in no condition to compete anymore. Given his spatial disorientation, he wasn't allowed to drive, so he never left the house, except, he says, to walk Kiana in her stroller.

These stroller walks around the neighborhood were supposed to help her fall asleep. Instead, she blinked awake and started gabbing away. They talked about music she liked, about her friends at school, about her favorite television shows. These walks became sacrosanct to Iram. When so many pieces of his life were coming apart, his time with Kiana made everything else fall away.

So when his friends finally convinced him to start racing again, Iram asked if he could bring Kiana along in a stroller.

The answer was yes, he could. But he faced a serious choice, one that would challenge his competitive nature and his goal to win. Running with his daughter was a nice idea, but it would increase his time. Running was a full-body workout. Add a twenty-five-pound buggy and forty-pound cargo, and he was going to be at a considerable disadvantage to runners otherwise unencumbered. The Iram everyone had known would never bow to such a handicap.

Before his cancer, before he'd realized he was dying, Iram ran to get better times because winning seemed like the most important thing in life. Winning still was important to him. Surely he wouldn't— *couldn't*—give up the prospect of a victory. But now winning wasn't the only thing that was meaningful to him. His relationship with Kiana was more important than ever. Running marathons with her in a stroller was an opportunity to spend quality time with her, to leave her with positive memories of their time together before he was gone. It seemed like an impossible choice, the outcome of which even his old teammates couldn't predict. Either way, Iram would be gaining something he valued enormously only to lose something he valued enormously.

For him, however, the choice was easy. "I'm only doing this if I can run with Kiana." He told his team he wasn't running to win anymore. Yes, it would be hard for him to leave that part of himself behind, but it was worth it. Kiana was worth it. He had always run to beat his time. Time was no longer something to beat. Time was something to cherish.

Today, if he walked the stroller across the finish line in last place at the Gusher Marathon, so be it.

Both Iram and Asha faced forks in the road, choices between two alternatives they powerfully valued. For Asha, driven by the impending need for surgery, the choice was between a skyrocketing career and her desire to be a mother. For Iram, it was a choice between using the precious time he had left either achieving athletic victories or spending as much time as possible with his daughter. Neither of their choices was easy, but for some reason, Iram made his more easily. While Asha deferred her decision, suffering the fear and regret that stemmed from that inaction, Iram committed fully to one alternative. Experts in the fields of psychology, marketing, and economics have long pondered why some people seem to get more easily caught in the net of decision paralysis than others.

Barry Schwartz, the Swarthmore professor we mentioned earlier, may have the solution. In his book *The Paradox of Choice*, he proposes that when it comes to making decisions, people fall into one of two camps: maximizers and satisficers. Maximizers aim to make the best choice possible. They may invest enormous amounts of effort and time fastidiously gathering as much information as possible about each option, considering all the alternatives and weighing all the pros and cons. The difficulty is that in today's world of almost boundless choices, the maximizer's task is never done. There's always more information to be gathered, more alternatives to be weighed. Satisficers, on the other hand, gather enough information to make a good-enough decision. Once they find an option that meets their needs, they stop and make the decision.

There is a significant trade-off between these two problem-solving styles. While maximizers objectively make better decisions than satisficers, they're less satisfied with their choices and often experience regret over the alternatives not chosen. Satisficers tend to be more content with their choices, though those choices may ultimately not be as good as the ones made by maximizers. This trade-off is vividly illustrated by a 2006 study published by Sheena Iyengar, Rachael Wells, and Barry Schwartz in the journal *Psychological Science*. They tracked hundreds of students from eleven universities in their senior year as they graduated and sought employment. Just before graduating, they were given a test of maximizing tendencies and asked questions about how they would go about seeking employment. A year later, the researchers followed up with the graduates, asking them whether they had found employment, what their starting salaries were, and how satisfied they felt with their jobs. Maximizers had secured objectively better jobs, at least if salary is any indication. They made $44,515 on average compared to satisficers' more meager $37,085. That's a 20 percent advantage. But maximizers were less happy with their choice of jobs, regretted that they didn't have more alternatives, tended to fantasize about having jobs other than those they had, and reported more negative feelings in general.

Iram, a satisficer, was content with his choice to run with his daughter. Everyone knew this meant leaving behind his chances of ever winning another race, but this sacrifice didn't torture him. He knew he couldn't have it all, realized there wasn't a perfect choice, and felt strongly that what he had was more than good enough. On the other hand, Asha, a maximizer, was objectively successful by anybody's standards. Her career had taken her into the world spotlight. She and her purple electric violin had toured with rock icons, and a major label had signed her band. But doubts and regrets about the options she had left behind tortured her. Like any good maximizer, she still wanted to have it all.

Asha woke on the morning of her thirty-fifth birthday in a small hotel room in Omaha, Nebraska. After Porcelain had concluded its tour, she returned to the United States to play with one of the top ten ticket-selling bands in the world, a progressive rock opera outfit called the Trans-Siberian Orchestra. Today she gazed out her hotel room window at the cars zipping past on Interstate 80. She imagined the drivers heading to work or dropping kids off at school, each person living lives far different from her own.

She showered, dressed, and drove her rental car to an empty arena where the Trans-Siberian Orchestra rehearses a couple of weeks every year before heading out on tour. It didn't feel like a birthday to Asha, and this was entirely by design. She would focus on work, on traveling, on the future. Still, the significance of today was inescapable.

As the age-thirty-five surgical deadline approached, Asha had felt the pressure mounting. She scrutinized the choices she'd made since becoming a supersurvivor and the life paths on which these choices had placed her. "Most of my friends back home look at my life and think, wow, it's so glamorous," Asha says. She knows from experience, however, that the life of an entertainer is not nearly as alluring as shows like *American Idol* want fans to believe. Hers is not a life of pampering and excess. Perhaps a few mega-successful entertainers live like royalty, but for Asha, life consisted of perpetual travel and a career that demanded nothing short of performing under tremendous scrutiny at a level of perfection. She'd given up the luxury of the familiar routine, of weekends off, of time with friends and family, of a place to call home, and of having the family she wanted. She wasn't rich, either. Not by a long shot.

Asha realized that entertainers get married and have children all the time. They also frequently adopt or have children on their own. Though she saw that having a child wouldn't mean giving up her career, she knew it would mean making sacrifices. In theory, she was willing to make compromises. In practice, however, Asha the maximizer was tortured by which compromises were the best to make. Motherhood isn't easy, and her values would demand that she be the very best mother she could. But being a touring rock violinist isn't easy, either, and her values were equally demanding here. She was haunted by the realization that no perfect solution was possible.

And the clock was ticking. The removal of her ovaries would mean losing the ability to choose when or if to have children.

We all face forks in the road, but maximizers such as Asha seem to feel an amplified sense of the gravity of loss that accompanies each choice, even with tremendous personal gain. More than a decade into remission, she was still facing difficult choices, and the most difficult one was still before her.

Asha tried not to make too much of her birthday and what it represented. The music, the rehearsal, and the prospect of a national arena tour with a new band provided her the best possible distraction. But there was no denying the march of time. At the end of rehearsal, the musicians came together and played "Happy Birthday" for her on the huge stage.

The melody stretched to the edges of the empty arena. The final notes held on for what seemed like an eternity. Asha had made up her mind not to call and schedule her surgery, not that year. Not yet. There was, she hoped, still time.

———

"When are we going to go faster?" Kiana asked her father.

With a grin, Iram glanced down at his daughter in the running stroller. "We're not going fast enough for you?"

"Faster," she said.

He picked up his speed.

Kiana looked at the scene around her. A long tire-black road. Thick, reaching branches of oak trees extending all around them.

There were no cars and no other runners. "Haven't we been here already?"

"We're running a double loop," Iram responded, glancing around.

The wind was growing stronger, adding strain to a route that was already difficult enough navigating with a stroller. Stroller running made quick hairpin turns impossible.

Still, Iram thought, *we're making good enough time.*

He and Kiana would finish the first loop at one hour and sixty minutes. Iram took off his headset and plugged his iPod into the little speaker he'd started using when he began taking Kiana along on runs.

Since his diagnosis two years before, he hadn't competed in a race without Kiana. He hadn't won any, either, though his times, surprisingly, hadn't been half bad. His teammates had long since acquiesced to Iram's choice to run with a stroller—a reasonable preference, but a choice he would not have made so easily before diagnosis, back when he was in the race to win.

He didn't think Kiana fully understood the concept of death yet, or that in a few years he wouldn't be there anymore. She'd found this out, though, when, in March of 2012, her father went on a training run and woke up in an ambulance again, having collapsed, unconscious. His physicians ran a battery of tests afterward and tripled his antiseizure medications on race days. Now when he trained, he wore a GPS device so people could monitor him. His spatial orientation was poor. He felt fine most of the time, but he was losing confidence in himself. Having Kiana there with him on these runs only made it better.

The iPod played a Randy Newman song from the movie *A Bug's Life.* Kiana started singing along. Iram joined in: *"It's the time of your life so live it well."*

The road turned sharply at the start of the second loop. At the bend, Iram looked behind him and saw a length of road without any runners, just as two volunteers appeared ahead. One offered Iram and Kiana snacks. He waved them away. "Give them to her." The biker tossed a banana, energy gels, and a bottle of water into the stroller.

"Hey," Iram said breathlessly to the biker. "How far behind am I?"

"No, man," the biker said. "There's no one ahead of you." The closest runner was six minutes behind them.

Impossible, thought Iram. *We're ahead?*

He pushed through his fatigue and found a good pace. At mile twenty-five he turned around again; he and Kiana were still alone on the road. Kiana was singing Bon Jovi's "Open Highway." She stopped singing when she noticed people on the sidelines cheering.

"Why are they shouting?"

The wind was pushing harder, and it was more difficult for Iram to breathe. He told her to be polite and wave to everyone.

"We're in first place," he said. "We're going to win."

He was certain now. The finish line was just a few yards ahead, and he had his cheerleader with him, pushing him toward victory as he pushed her.

The *Beaumont Enterprise* newspaper reported that a man with terminal cancer had won the marathon. Iram's story was too good not to be featured on the front page. Local television and radio news reported his victory, which would have been impressive enough even if he hadn't won the race while pushing his young daughter in a stroller. Just as with Alan Lock's victorious row across the Atlantic Ocean and Maarten van der Weijden's triumph from illness to Olympic gold, people were quick to attribute Iram's victory to the so-called "power of positive thinking." But we know there's much more at work than mere positive thinking; these stories are full of anguish and struggle. *The Wall Street Journal* ran a feature-length piece on Iram, implying that he was a hero: "He won the Gusher Marathon, finishing in 3:07:35. That was one second slower than his personal record in the 26.2-mile event, set days before he underwent brain surgery in early 2011 . . . Leon's high-speed finish provides cancer survivors with an athletic role model only weeks after the defrocking of Austin's more-famous cancer-battling competitor, Lance Armstrong."

Iram blanches when he reads these kinds of comparisons, because he doesn't feel like a hero. "If anything, I feel I should have started running with my daughter sooner," he says. "I have friends who've had to relearn to walk and talk and have also run marathons, and lung cancer survivors who struggle to breathe. These are the heroes. I run because things still work. Most of us know what we need to get through the day, to be better athletes, better parents, better friends. I've found that most of us aren't lacking information, we're lacking inspiration."

People, Iram finds, are impressed with the choice he made, but for him, it just seemed like the right thing to do.

———

Asha's performance on the electric violin was a centerpiece of the Trans-Siberian Orchestra's highly theatrical symphonic fusion of classical music set to heavy metal, bombastic lasers, and pulsating lights. Now age thirty-six, she and the Trans-Siberian Orchestra released a five-song EP that debuted at number one on *Billboard*'s Top 200 Rock Chart. To support the EP, they planned an arena tour of sixty cities in three months.

On the final night of that 2012 tour, the arena lights came down and the darkness was spliced by a single beam of blue that became dozens of green streaks skating across fifteen thousand fans. While playing, Asha ran through the audience to the back of the arena. She took her place on a movable platform that swiftly rose thirty feet above the crowd against an explosion of pyrotechnics igniting behind and below her. At the finale, she made her way back to the main stage, which was backlit by towering walls of video screens. Along the way, she stopped to play her electric violin to a group of kids at stage left. The arena was ablaze with music and lights that culminated in bursts of white fireworks. In those final moments, the temperature onstage jumped fifteen degrees, and Asha, in grand theatricality, broke her bow across her knee.

Backstage, she signed autographs for fans and then jumped back on the tour bus, which took her to the hotel. In the morning, she would take a flight to Boston to visit her family and once again consider her next move. In twenty-four hours it was going to be New Year's Eve, time once again to make new promises to herself and think about the choices her life presented. She might take a trip to the Middle East with friends or enroll in a ten-day silent meditation program. She might go to Washington, DC, to shoot a twelve-episode pilot for the Travel Channel or move back to Los Angeles and play violin with *The Tonight Show* band again. The future seemed limitless.

Before making up her mind, in the winter of 2013 she visited Beth Israel Deaconess Medical Center in Boston. Her oncologist had reluctantly gone along with her decision to put off the surgery, as long as Asha submitted to a genetic test for mutations of tumor suppressors called BRCA1 and BRCA2. A mutation would indicate a particularly strong risk of her developing ovarian cancer. Ruling out this vulnerability would make her medical team much more comfortable with her decision to wait. If the tests indicated particular abnormalities, however, her oncologist would urge Asha not to wait a moment longer to schedule the surgery.

A nurse came into the examination room and passed Asha a plastic vial to fill with saliva. Asha held the vial in her fingers as she would a violin bow, filled it the best she could, and handed it back. The nurse took the small tube from her and left the room. Asha gazed at her knees and struggled to catch her breath. A decade of performing live in front of millions of people had given her nerves of steel, but they melted under the threat of what this test might tell her about her body.

The results were late. Asha called the clinic and was told the sample she'd given had somehow been contaminated. So she repeated the test.

In the waning days of the summer of 2013, Asha learned that she did not have the particular markers that indicated an increased risk for ovarian cancer. Though she is not entirely free of risk, she could much more safely wait until age forty to have the surgery, an age when fertility for most women naturally drops to very low levels. She still had a little time to settle down, to meet someone, and to start a family. If that did not happen, she says, she would pursue alternative methods of fertility, such as egg freezing and *in vitro* fertilization.

"I've made choices in my life. Not good or bad choices, just decisions that were right for me at the time," Asha says. "I would love to tell you that I have everything I want right now." She thinks for a moment. "But I definitely don't have regrets. . . . I wouldn't change any of the decisions I made."

Like Asha, Iram, and all the survivors we've met along the way, every one of us must play the cards we've been dealt. As much as we might yearn for a life without pain, without suffering, without adversity, we realize we're asking the impossible. We must make choices—sometimes difficult, sometimes easy—based on what life puts in front of us. But we know how to survive these trials, and how to thrive despite them—or perhaps because of them. It's part of who we are. Life is worth embracing in part because of our ability to transform suffering into triumph and setbacks into successes. Supersurvival isn't a magic bullet that makes everything instantly better. It's not something we do that solves all our problems forever. In a way, life is a constant process of supersurvival, of facing life's seemingly impossible choices with honesty and faith in ourselves. It's a capacity all of us share.

It's the capacity to hope.

Epilogue

On August 10, 1976, a thirty-three-year-old working-class mother left her house in Belfast to run errands. For roughly ten years the city had been a theater of violent clashes between the mostly Protestant unionists eager to keep Northern Ireland with the United Kingdom and the mostly Catholic nationalists fighting to create a united Ireland. For residents such as Betty Williams, a quiet receptionist with shoulder-length dark hair and a toothy smile, political violence, riots, and bombings punctuated ordinary life. On her drive into town that sunny afternoon, as she turned the corner onto Finaghy Road, the *thud, thud, thud* of British army rifles rang out.

Just ahead, two Irish Republican Army operators were fleeing British troops in a stolen blue Ford. As the Ford raced through the residential neighborhood, another shot rang out, piercing the vehicle's hull and instantly killing Danny Lennon, the driver. For the rest of her life, Betty Williams would be haunted by what happened in the next five seconds. The Ford, now driverless and out of control, jumped the curb and crashed into a young mother who was out for a walk with her three young children. Betty leapt from her car to help, but quickly discovered there was little she could do. Though the mother had survived, her three children, one of them only six weeks old, would die. Betty would never be able to blot out the memory of their screams, of their mangled bodies, of the blood.

Betty did not know the children Joanne, John, and Andrew Maguire, but their deaths would propel her life in an entirely new direction. Before that day, she was not politically active; nor had she ever taken any stand on the Troubles in Northern Ireland. Yet the horrible events on Finaghy Road sparked something within her. She could no longer sit idly by while such senseless violence pulled more innocents into the line of fire.

Two days after the tragedy, Betty took to the streets. She knocked on door after door, pleaded with person after person, and acquired six thousand signatures on a petition to denounce the actions of the IRA and demand peace on both sides. Her actions caught the attention of the aunt of the three dead children, Máiread Corrigan, who invited Betty to the funerals. Soon after, both women were scheduled to appear on a local television news show. There, Betty and Máiread met another guest, a Northern Ireland correspondent for *The Irish Press* named Ciaran McKeown. Backstage, these three like-minded strangers connected, planting the seeds of an alliance that would play a crucial role in ending the violence in Northern Ireland. Over the next thirty years, their grassroots organization, the Community of Peace People, would fight for human rights, support interfaith schools, create peace camps, and petition for nonviolent approaches to conflict resolution.

But first, Peace People would give voice to the three children of the Maguire family, lost forever. "I called the local newspaper and told them we were asking the women of Ireland to join in a rally," Betty remembers. "The editor says to hold the front page, and puts my name on it, along with my address. We had no concept of what was just about to happen." On the night of the rally, buses from both the Protestant and Catholic sides of town streamed into the site where the children were killed. Ten thousand women stepped off those buses and into each other's arms. Betty had never known healing like this in her life. "It was as though someone had brushed out more than eight hundred years of bad history," she says.

Within days of the march, Betty and her collaborators organized a second rally, this one attracting more than thirty thousand people.

When we began writing this book, we set out to explore the legacy of trauma.

Long fascinated and inspired by human beings' ability to bounce back from tragedy, we read hundreds of research studies on the topic and conducted more than a hundred interviews. Frankly, we expected most survivors to paint a grim picture. Understandably, many victims of trauma are emotionally overwhelmed by their experiences. Some are plagued by nightmares or overcome by fear.

The stories of people who suffer mightily from trauma are important. But we wanted to give voice to a different kind of story that people rarely hear. We wanted to learn from the experience of those who had encountered fundamental, life-altering growth in response to trauma and, as a result, had revolutionized their lives and often the world around them. We realized that if we were going to illustrate the principles that help people do this, we were going to have to find solid examples of such dramatic transformation.

At first we thought we'd be searching for a needle in a haystack. We were wrong—and were both surprised and enthralled by the incredible stories we encountered.

After two successful marches in Belfast, hundreds of thousands of people joined Peace People's movement. To understand the significance of this remarkable feat, consider Northern Ireland's more recent history. In 1964, when Betty was twenty-one years old, she witnessed the emergence of a civil rights movement to end discrimination against the mostly Catholic nationalist minority. The unwelcoming and sometimes violent response this movement received from elements of the mostly Protestant pro-British majority ignited a rise in violence by the Provisional Irish Republican Army, a paramilitary group whose goal was the independence of Northern Ireland from Great Britain. In the 1970s, Betty's city of Belfast became home to some of the worst unemployment, violence, and political strife in the Western world. Most people hoped that eventually the anger and violence would diminish and neighbors would be able to work together. Yet it took a few very special people such as Betty Williams and Máiread Corrigan to truly bring people together.

People tend to look at Betty Williams with a sense of awe. But the woman who stood against the cycle of violence in Northern Ireland believes that anyone could have stepped in to do what she did. "I hate to use the word *ordinary*, but I was just ordinary," says Betty. "I was a happy woman with a lovely wee home, a car, a headband, and kids. I was content with my home, but not with what was happening on the streets of Belfast. I tried to live some kind of normality in a war situation. That's all I did."

To the outside world, Betty seemed somehow gifted with exactly the right combination of almost superhuman abilities and skills to get the job done. Who else besides Betty could bring together warring parties, salve decades-old wounds, and heal a hemorrhaging society? But Betty insists that she isn't special.

This denial isn't false humility. Betty truly believes that anyone in her position would have done exactly the same thing. As we interviewed supersurvivor after supersurvivor in preparation to write this book, we began to see that Betty wasn't alone. Every tale of supersurvivorship began with an ordinary person living an ordinary life. And almost every one of our survivors insisted that we clearly and pointedly communicate this fact. Ordinary people can do extraordinary things.

In 1976 Betty was giving a talk to an audience in London at the Savoy Hotel. Afterward, she walked to the lobby, where a young man approached her.

"Congratulations, Miss Williams," he said.

Betty looked oddly at the boy. She hadn't yet heard.

"Ma'am," he said, "you've just been awarded the Nobel Peace Prize."

Betty Williams and Máiread Corrigan were to be joint recipients of the coveted prize for their work with the Community of Peace People. Betty could hardly believe it. A year earlier, she was a receptionist. Today, she was among the most famous agents of change in the world.

And yet, as excited and honored as she was to win the award, she was conflicted. She didn't believe that she deserved it. She believed that anyone could have accomplished what she had. The only difference was that she, like other supersurvivors, decided to change her life after experiencing something horrible.

Throughout this book, we've seen that the otherwise destructive forces of trauma can sometimes initiate dramatic positive transformation. But is it really necessary to suffer in order to experience this magnitude of change?

We posed this question to Betty. "One day I was sitting in my office and a group of prostitutes came to see me," she responded. "One hands me a check for a hundred pounds. They didn't know these children. But they cared. They lived here, too," she says. "Pain will change you. It does change you. But so does knowledge."

Betty decided that accepting the Nobel Prize would allow her to open new doors for the cause, spreading knowledge around the world to those who needed it. That included many people who had never experienced the conflict in Northern Ireland up close, but who could find within themselves the desire to change their lives and maybe the lives of others.

"I accepted this award on behalf of every woman in Northern Ireland who worked, sang, and walked for peace," Betty says.

We intended to write a book about how a few extraordinary people had survived trauma. With the help of supersurvivors such as Betty, however, we ended up writing about how every one of us can live more fully. From Alan Lock, Maarten van der Weijden, and Casey Pieretti we learned a new way of rooting positive thinking in a brave and honest understanding of reality. From Paul Rieckhoff and Cindy Sheehan we learned the value of questioning even our most precious assumptions. From Paul Watkins and Candy Chang we learned that to live meaningfully and completely sometimes means admitting that we eventually will die. From James Cameron and Michael Bussee we learned that faith can bring both deep blessings and great burdens. From Aaron Acharya and Clemantine Wamariya we learned how forgiveness can be personally empowering. From Amanda Wigal and Jane McGonigal we learned the value of opening ourselves to the love and support of others. And from Asha Mevlana and Iram Leon we learned not to waste the precious choices life offers.

From each we learned that it is possible to brave life's trials with a deep sense of hope, and that, rooted in the act of confronting the entanglements of life, every one of us has the capacity to be super.

Acknowledgments

We cannot adequately measure the weight of our gratitude to the survivors who lent their voices and their experiences to this book. We were overwhelmed by their willingness to open up about their lives, have been personally touched by their ordeals and their triumphs, and are honored to be entrusted with their uniquely harrowing stories.

In addition, we extend our special thanks to Dan Farley, a man of considerable generosity of spirit and sage guidance. We are deeply grateful to Richard Pine, whose council creates a particular sort of alchemy that turns ideas into reality and agents into comrades. The same can be said for the fine people at Inkwell Management, especially David Hale Smith, Alexis Hurley, Lizz Blaise, Nathaniel Jacks, and Eliza Rothstein. We reserve a special acknowledgment for Karen Rinaldi, our incredible editor, who defined, and then re-defined, resilience for us. Our appreciation extends to her staff, Jake Zebede, Julie Will, Stephanie Cooper, Steven Boriack, and the entire team at HarperCollins—in particular HarperWave, an imprint with the exhilarating goal of changing readers' lives.

Mimi Kravetz and Vin Eiamvuthikorn quite literally endured years of listening to us talk "book," and their patience and wisdom remain our secret ingredient. Additional thanks goes out to Janis Cooke Newman, whose encouragement cultivated a seed of an idea into this book, as well as to Ethan Watters, Po Bronson, Stacy Perman, and Ellen Geiger.

We are grateful to our families, Jim and Terri Kravetz, and Michael and Pamela Feldman, who instilled in us a deep curiosity about the world. Additional thanks go out to Ryan Elliot Kravetz, Carin and Paul Feldman, Vicki Tsi, Liora Bowers, Lilach Shafir, Tony D'souza, Mona Kerby, Dina Nayeri, and Daniel Steven, who provided foundational support.

We were humbled by the generous backing of people and organizations, including John Carpenter, Adam Savage, Dan Tapster, M5 Industries, the Desmond Tutu Peace Foundation, AMP'D Gear, the Before I Die Project, and The Bucket List Foundation. Further thanks go to the International Paralympic Committee, the Sigi Ziering Institute, Lucky Duck Productions, the NYU Cancer Center, America's Black Holocaust Museum, the Iraq Afganistan Veterans of America, Stanford University Hospital and Clinics, *Psychology Today, The Huffington Post*, Cancer Care of New York, the NYU Clinical Cancer Center, Johns Hopkins University Hospital, and Gopi Kallayil at Google Inc.

We wrote much of this book as inhabitants of the San Francisco Writer's Grotto. Spaces have souls, and the Grotto's overflows its confines of brick and mortar.

References

CHAPTER 1

Affleck, G., H. Tennen, S. Croog, and S. Levine. "Causal Attribution, Perceived Benefits, and Morbidity after a Heart Attack: An 8-Year Study." *Journal of Consulting and Clinical Psychology* 55 (1987): 29–35.

American Cancer Society. *Global Cancer: Facts and Figures,* 2nd ed. Atlanta, GA: American Cancer Society, 2008.

Bonnano, G. A., and E. D. Diminich. "Annual Research Review: Positive Adjustment to Adversity—Trajectories of Minimal-Impact Resilience and Emergent Resilience." *The Journal of Child Psychology and Psychiatry* 54 (2013): 378–401.

Bonnano, G. A., S. Galea, A. Bucciarelli, and D. Vlahov. "What Predicts Psychological Resilience after Disaster? The Role of Demographics, Resources, and Life Stress." *Journal of Consulting and Clinical Psychology* 75 (2007): 671–82.

Calhoun, L. G., and R. G. Tedeschi. *Facilitating Posttraumatic Growth: A Clinician's Guide.* Mahwah, NJ: Erlbaum, 1999.

Costanzo, E. S., C. D. Ryff, and B. H. Singer. "Psychosocial Adjustment among Cancer Survivors: Findings from a National Survey of Health and Well-Being." *Health Psychology* 28 (2009): 147–56.

Dabney, L. "Polar Vision Expedition to Set Antarctic Record." *The Faster*

Times, October 27, 2011. http://www.thefastertimes.com/news/ 2011/10/27/polar-vision-expedition-to-set-antarctic-record/.

Davis, C. G., S. Nolen-Hoeksema, and J. Larson. "Making Sense of Loss and Benefiting from the Experience: Two Construals of Meaning." *Journal of Personality and Social Psychology* 75 (1998): 561–74.

Elder, G. H., and E. C. Clipp. "Combat Experience and Emotional Health: Impairment and Resilience in Later Life." *Journal of Personality* 57 (1989): 311–41.

Fontana, A., and R. Rosenheck. "Psychological Benefits and Liabilities of Traumatic Exposure in the War Zone." *Journal of Traumatic Stress* 11 (1998): 485–503.

Frazier, P., A. Conlon, and T. Glaser. "Positive and Negative Life Changes Following Sexual Assault." *Journal of Consulting and Clinical Psychology* 69 (2001): 1048–55.

Frazier, P., N. Keenan, S. Anders, S. Perera, S. Shallcross, and S. Hintz. "Perceived Past, Present, and Future Control and Adjustment to Stressful Life Events." *Journal of Personality and Social Psychology* 100, no. 4 (2011): 749–65.

Frazier, P., H. Tennen, M. Gavian, C. Park, P. Tomich, and T. Tashiro. "Does Self-Reported Posttraumatic Growth Reflect Genuine Positive Change?" *Psychological Science* 20 (2009): 912–19.

Gean, A. D., and N. J. Fischbein. "Head Trauma." *Neuroimaging Clinics of North America* 20, no. 4 (2010): 527–56.

Gernsbacher, M. A., R. W. Pew, L. M. Hough, and J. R. Pomerantz. *Psychology and the Real World: Essays Illustrating Fundamental Contributions to Society.* New York: Worth Publishers, 2011.

Gunty, A. L., P. A. Frazier, H. Tennen, P. Tomich, T. Tashiro, and C. Park. "Moderators of the Relation between Perceived and Actual Posttraumatic Growth." *Psychological Trauma: Theory, Research, Practice, and Policy* 3 (2011): 61–66.

Helgeson, V. S., K. A. Reynolds, and P. L. Tomich. "A Meta-Analytic Review of Benefit Finding and Growth." *Journal of Consulting and Clinical Psychology* 74 (2006): 797–816.

Herman, J. *Trauma and Recovery: The Aftermath of Violence from Domestic Abuse to Political Terror.* New York: Basic Books, 1992.

Kessler, R. C., A. Sonnega, E. Bromet, M. Hughes, and C. B. Nelson. "Posttraumatic Stress Disorder in the National Comorbidity Survey." *Archives of General Psychiatry* 52 (1995): 1048–60.

Linley, P. A., and S. Joseph. "Positive Change Following Trauma and Adversity." *Journal of Traumatic Stress* 17 (2004): 11–21.

McMillen, J. C., E. M. Smith, and R. H. Fisher. "Perceived Benefit and Mental Health after Three Types of Disaster." *Journal of Consulting and Clinical Psychology* 65 (1997): 733–39.

Norris, F. H, M. J. Friedman, P. J. Watson, C. M. Byrne, E. Diaz, and K. Kaniasty. "60,000 Disaster Victims Speak—Part I: An Empirical Review of the Empirical Literature, 1981–2001." *Psychiatry: Interpersonal and Biological Processes* 65 (2002): 207–39.

Pollard, C., and P. Kennedy. "A Longitudinal Analysis of Emotional Impact, Coping Strategies and Post-Traumatic Psychological Growth Following Spinal Cord Injury: A 10-Year Review." *British Journal of Health Psychology* 12 (2007): 347–62.

Sims, T. "Trekking beyond Limits in Antarctica. *The New York Times*, October 21, 2011. http://www.nytimes.com/2011/10/22/sports/22iht-athlete22.html?_r=0.

Tedeschi, R. G., and L. G. Calhoun. "The Posttraumatic Growth Inventory: Measuring the Positive Legacy of Trauma." *Journal of Traumatic Stress* 9 (1996): 455–71.

———. "Posttraumatic Growth: Conceptual Foundations and Empirical Evidence." *Psychological Inquiry* 15 (2004): 1–18.

Vrana, S., and D. Lauterbach. "Prevalence of Traumatic Events and Post-Traumatic Psychological Symptoms in a Nonclinical Sample of College Students." *Journal Traumatic Stress* 7 (1994): 289–302.

United Nations Development Fund for Women. "Unite to End Violence against Women: United Nations Secretary-General's Campaign," New York, 2008. http://www.un.org/en/women/endviolence/world.shtml.

World Health Organization. "Road Traffic Injuries." Geneva, 2013. http://www.who.int/mediacentre/factsheets/fs358/en/.

Zolli, A., and A. M. Healy. *Resilience: Why Things Bounce Back.* New York: Free Press, 2012.

CHAPTER 2

Armstrong, L. *It's Not about the Bike: My Journey Back to Life.* New York: Berkley Trade, 2001.

Braver, R., senior correspondent. "Just How Powerful Is Positive Thinking?" [television broadcast]. *CBS Sunday Morning*, November 22, 2011.

Buckelew, S. P., R. S. Crittendon, J. D. Butkovic, K. B. Price, and M. Hurst. "Hope as a Predictor of Academic Performance." *Psychological Reports* 103 (2008): 411–14.

Cheavens, J. S., D. B. Feldman, A. Gum, S. T. Michael, and C. R. Snyder. "Hope Therapy in a Community Sample: A Pilot Investigation." *Social Indicators Research* 77 (2006): 61–78.

Chida, Y., and A. Steptoe. "Positive Psychological Well-Being and Mortality: A Quantitative Review of Prospective Observational Studies." *Psychosomatic Medicine* 70 (2008): 741–56.

Coyne, J. C. "Was It Shown That 'Close Relationships and Emotional Processing Predict Decreased Mortality in Women with Breast Cancer'? A Critique of Weihs et al." *Psychosomatic Medicine* 70 (2008): 737.

Coyne, J. C., T. F. Pajak, J. Harris, A. Konski, B. Movsas, K. Ang, and D. W. Bruner. "Emotional Well-Being Does Not Predict Survival in Head and Neck Cancer Patients: A Radiation Therapy Oncology Group Study." *Cancer* 110 (2007): 2568–75.

Coyne, J. C., M. Stefanek, and S. C. Palmer. "Psychotherapy and Survival in Cancer: The Conflict between Hope and Evidence." *Psychological Bulletin* 133 (2007): 367–94.

Coyne, J. C., H. Tennen, and A. V. Ranchor. "Positive Psychology in Cancer Care: A Story Line Resistant to Evidence." *Annals of Behavioral Medicine* 39 (2010): 35–42.

Curry, L. A., C. R. Snyder, D. L. Cook, B. C. Ruby, and M. Rehm. "Role of Hope in Academic and Sport Achievement." *Journal of Personality and Social Psychology* 73 (1997): 1257–67.

Ehrenreich, B. *Bright-Sided: How Positive Thinking Is Undermining America*. New York: Henry Holt, 2009.

Feldman, D. B., and D. E. Dreher. "Can Hope Be Changed in 90 Minutes? Testing the Efficacy of a Single-Session Goal-Pursuit Intervention for College Students." *Journal of Happiness Studies* 13 (2012): 745–59.

Feldman, D. B., K. L. Rand, and K. Kahle-Wrobleski. "Hope and Goal Attainment: Testing a Basic Prediction of Hope Theory." *Journal of Social and Clinical Psychology* 28 (2009): 479–97.

Feldman, D. B., and C. R. Snyder. "Hope and the Meaningful Life: Theoretical and Empirical Associations between Goal-Directed Thinking and Life Meaning." *Journal of Social and Clinical Psychology* 24 (2005): 401–21.

Gallagher, B. "Maarten van der Weijden: Don't Call Me Lance Armstrong." *The Daily Telegraph*, August 21, 2008. http://www.telegraph.co.uk/sport/olympics/2594982/ Maarten-van-der-Weijden-Dont-call-me-Lance-Armstrong.html.

Goodwin, P., M. Leszcz, M. Ennis, J. Koopmans, L. Vincent, H. Guther, and J. Hunter. "The Effects of Group Psychosocial Support on Survival in Metastatic Breast Cancer." *The New England Journal of Medicine* 345 (2001): 1719–26.

Gore-Felton, C., and D. Spiegel. "Enhancing Women's Lives: The Role of Support Groups among Breast Cancer Patients." *Journal for Specialists in Group Work* 24 (2008): 274–87.

Heckhausen, J., C. Wrosch, and W. Fleeson. "Developmental Regulation before and after a Developmental Deadline: The Sample Case of 'Biological Clock' for Childbearing." *Psychology and Aging* 16 (2001): 400–13.

Hull, S. J. "Perceived Risk as a Moderator of the Effectiveness of Framed HIV-Test Promotion Messages among Women: A Randomized Controlled Trial." *Health Psychology* 31 (2012): 114–21.

Irving, L. M., C. R. Snyder, and J. Cheavens. "The Relationships between Hope and Outcomes at the Pretreatment, Beginning, and Later Phases of Psychotherapy." *Journal of Psychotherapy Integration* 14 (2004): 419–43.

Janz, N. K., and M. H. Becker. "The Health Belief Model: A Decade Later." *Health Education Quarterly* 11 (1984): 1–47.

Lieven, P., W. Frank, B. Gerben, and W. Bernasco. "Perceived Sanction Risk, Individual Propensity and Adolescent Offending: Assessing Key Findings from the Deterrence Literature in a Dutch Sample." *European Journal of Criminology* 8 (2011): 386–400.

Miller, G. E., and C. Wrosch. "You've Gotta Know When to Fold 'Em: Goal Disengagement and Systemic Inflammation in Adolescence." *Psychological Science* 18 (2007): 773–77.

Moser, R. P., K. McCaul, E. Peters, W. Nelson, and S. E. Marcus. "Associations of Perceived Risk and Worry with Cancer Health-Protective Actions." *Journal of Health Psychology* 12 (2007): 53–65.

Neter, E., A. Litvak, and A. Miller. "Goal Disengagement and Goal Re-Engagement among Multiple Sclerosis Patients: Relationship to Well-Being and Illness Representation." *Psychological Health* 24 (2009): 175–86.

Oceanrowing.com. "Completed Ocean Rows in Chronological Order of Departures," 2010. http://www.oceanrowing.com/statistics/stats_rows_chronological_order.htm.

Peale, N. M. *The Power of Positive Thinking*. New York: Prentice-Hall, 1952.

Schweingruber, D. "Success through a Positive Mental Attitude? The Role of Positive Thinking in Door-to-Door Sales." *The Sociological Quarterly* 47 (2006): 41–68.

Snyder, C. R., D. B. Feldman, J. D. Taylor, J. D., L. L. Schroeder, and V. Adams III. "The Roles of Hopeful Thinking in Preventing Problems and Promoting Strengths." *Applied and Preventive Psychology: Current Scientific Perspectives* 15 (2000): 262–95.

Snyder, C. R., C. Harris, J. R. Anderson, S. A. Holleran, L. M. Irving, S. T. Sigmon, et al. "The Will and the Ways: Development and Validation of an Individual-Differences Measure of Hope." *Journal of Personality and Social Psychology* 60 (1991): 570–85.

Spiegel, D. *Living beyond Limits: New Hope and Healing for Facing Life-Threatening Illness*. New York: Random House, 1995.

van der Weijden, M. *Better*. Netherlands: Ambo, 2010.

———. "On Surviving Cancer and Becoming Olympic Champion." Presentation delivered at TEDx, Rotterdam, September 9, 2010. http://tedxtalks.ted.com/video/TEDxRotterdam-Maarten -van-der-W.

Weinstein, N. D., A. Kwitel, K. D. McCaul, R. E. Magnan, M. Gerrard, and F. X. Gibbons. "Risk Perceptions: Assessment and Relationship to Influenza Vaccination." *Health Psychology* 26 (2007): 146–51.

Weiss, R. *The American Myth of Success: From Horatio Alger to Norman Vincent Peale*. Champaign: University of Illinois Press, 1988.

Wrosch, C., M. F. Scheier, C. S. Carver, and R. Schulz. "The Importance of Goal Disengagement in Adaptive Self-Regulation: When Giving Up Is Beneficial." *Self and Identity* 2 (2003): 1–20.

CHAPTER 3

Brown, S. L., and R. V. Gould. "A Prospective Study of Relationships between Propositions about Risk and Driver Speeding." *Accident Analysis and Prevention* 46 (2012): 1–7.

Goldsmith M. "Helping Successful People Get Even Better." *Business Strategy Review* 14 (2003): 9–16.

Goldsmith, M., and M. Reiter. *What Got You Here Won't Get You There*. New York: Hyperion, 2007.

Hallett, C., A. Lambert, and M. A. Regan. "Text Messaging amongst New Zealand Drivers: Prevalence and Risk Perception." *Transportation Research*, Part F, 15 (2012): 261–71.

James, N. J., P. A. Gillies, and C. J. Bignell. "AIDS-Related Risk Perception and Sexual Behaviour among Sexually Transmitted Disease Clinic Attenders." *International Journal of STD and AIDS* 2 (1991): 264–71.

Janz, N. K., and M. H. Becker. "The Health Belief Model: A Decade Later." *Health Education Quarterly* 11 (1984): 1–47.

Lowther, J., and H. Lane. "Self-Efficacy and Psychological Skills during the Amputee Soccer World Cup." *Athletic Insight: The Online Journal of Sports Psychology* 4 (2002). http://www.athleticinsight.com/Vol4Iss2/SoccerSelfEfficacy.htm.

Nelson, E., P. Atchley, P., and T. D. Little. "The Effects of Perception of Risk and Importance of Answering and Initiating a Cellular Phone Call While Driving." *Accident Analysis and Prevention* 41 (2009): 438–44.

Olson, R. L., R. J. Hanowski, J. S. Hickman, and J. Bocanegra. *Driver Distraction in Commercial Vehicle Operators*. Washington, DC: U.S. Department of Transportation, 2009.

Taylor, S. E. *Positive Illusions: Creative Self-Deception and the Healthy Mind*. New York: Basic Books, 1991.

Taylor, S. E., and D. A. Armor. "Positive Illusions and Coping with Adversity." *Journal of Personality* 64 (1996): 873–98.

Weinberger, M., J. Y. Greene, J. J. Mamlin, and M. J. Jerin. "Health Beliefs and Smoking Behavior. *American Journal of Public Health* 71 (1981): 1253–55.

Weinstein, N. D. "Unrealistic Optimism about Future Life Events." *Journal of Personality and Social Psychology* 39 (1980): 806–20.

CHAPTER 4

Draper, R. S. Goldstein, W. S. Hylton, M. Kirby, R. Naddaf, T. Newmyer, and G. Veis. "The 50 Most Powerful People in D.C." *GQ*, November 2009. http://www.gq.com/news-politics/politics/200911/50-most-powerful-people-in-dc#slide=1.

Janoff-Bulman, R. "Assumptive Worlds and the Stress of Traumatic Events: Applications of the Schema Construct." *Social Cognition* 7 (1989): 113–36.

———. *Shattered Assumptions: Towards a New Psychology of Trauma*. New York: Free Press, 2002.

Joseph, S. *What Doesn't Kill Us: The New Psychology of Posttraumatic Growth*. New York: Basic Books, 2011.

Joseph, S., and P. A. Linley. "Positive Adjustment to Threatening Events: An Organismic Valuing Theory of Growth through Adversity." *Review of General Psychology* 9 (2005): 262–80.

Lerner, M. J. *The Belief in a Just World: A Fundamental Delusion*. New York: Springer, 1980.

———. "The Justice Motive: Where Social Psychologists Found It, How They Lost It, and Why They Might Not Find It Again." *Personality and Social Psychology Review* 7 (2003): 388–99.

———. "Observer's Evaluation of a Victim: Justice, Guilt, and Veridical Perception." *Journal of Personality and Social Psychology* 20 (1971): 17–35.

Littleton, H. L., and A. Grills-Taquechel. "Evaluation of an Information-Processing Model Following Sexual Assault." *Psychological Trauma: Theory, Research, Practice, and Policy* 3 (2011): 421–29.

Matthews, C. (host). *Hardball with Chris Matthews*, MSNBC, August 23, 2005.

Morgan, G. S., D. C. Wisneski, and L. J. Skitka. "The Expulsion from Disneyland: The Social Psychological Impact of 9/11." *American Psychologist* 66 (2011): 447–54.

Payne, A. J., S. Joseph, and J. Tudway. "Assimilation and Accommodation Processes Following Traumatic Experiences." *Journal of Loss and Trauma* 12 (2007): 73–89.

Resick, P. A., and M. K. Schnicke. "Cognitive Processing Therapy for Sexual Assault Victims." *Journal of Consulting and Clinical Psychology* 60 (1992): 748–56.

Rieckhoff, P. *Chasing Ghosts: Failures and Facades in Iraq: A Soldier's Perspective*. New York: NAL, 2007.

———. "The Iraq Debate—New Ideas Series, Volume 1: "The Gelb/Biden Plan." *Huffington Post*, June 15, 2006. http://www.huffingtonpost.com/paul-rieckhoff/the-iraq-debatenew-ideas-_b_23061.html.

Sheehan, C. "A Bright Spot in Bush World amid the Miserable Failures on the Same Planet." *Huffington Post*, September 16, 2005. http://www.huffingtonpost.com/cindy-sheehan/a-bright-spot-in-bush-wor_b_7433.html.

———. *Myth America: 10 Greatest Myths of the Robber Class and the Case for Revolution*. San Francisco, CA: Cindy Sheehan's Soapbox, LLC, 2009.

———. *Not One More Mother's Child*. Maui, HI: Koa Books, 2005.

CHAPTER 5

Brewin, C. R., B. Andrews, and J. D. Valentine. "Meta-Analysis of Risk Factors for Posttraumatic Stress Disorder in Trauma-Exposed Adults." *Journal of Consulting and Clinical Psychology* 68 (2000): 748–66.

Corbett, P. "Scottsdale Chefs Endure Hard Times during Recession." *Arizona Republic*, January 29, 2000. http://www.azcentral.com/community/scottsdale/articles/20110129scottsdale-chefs-close-restaurants.html.

Gabert-Quillen, C. A., L. A. Irish, E. Sledjeski, E. Fallon, E. Spoonster, and D. L. Delahanty. "The Impact of Social Support on the

Relationship between Trauma History and Posttraumatic Stress Disorder in Motor Vehicle Accident Victims." *International Journal of Stress Management* 19 (2012): 69–79.

Goodwin, S. (executive producer). "Aid Worker Leaves Haiti with a Sour Taste" [radio broadcast]. *Talk of the Nation*. NPR. May 10, 2012.

Henderson, N. "Economy Gained Strength in 2006: Growth Dispels Recession Fears." *Washington Post*, February 1, 2007. http://www.washingtonpost.com/wp-dyn/content/article/2007/01/31/AR2007013100422.html.

Herbst-Damm, K., and J. Kulik. "Volunteer Support, Marital Status, and the Survival Times of Terminally Ill Patients." *Health Psychology* 24 (2005): 225–29.

Isidore, C. "It's Official: Recession since Dec. '07." *CNN Money*, December 1, 2008. http://money.cnn.com/2008/12/01/news/economy/recession/index.htm.

Kanani, R. "Gaming for Social Change: An In-Depth Interview with Jane McGonigal." *Forbes*, 2011. http://www.forbes.com/sites/rahimkanani/2011/09/19/gaming-for-social-change-an-in-depth-interview-with-jane-mcgonigal/.

Kaniasty, K., and F. Norris. "Mobilization and Deterioration of Social Support Following Natural Disasters." *Current Directions in Psychological Science* 4 (1995): 94–98.

Kress, A. "Phoenix Has Long Road Back to Recover Lost Jobs from Recession." *Phoenix Business Journal*, January 15, 2013. http://www.bizjournals.com/phoenix/news/2013/01/15/phoenix-has-long-road-back-to-recover.html.

McDowell, T. L., and J. M. Serovich. "The Effect of Perceived and Actual Social Support on the Mental Health of HIV-Positive Persons." *AIDS Care* 19 (2007): 1223–29.

McGonigal, J. "Jane McGonigal: The Game That Can Give You 10 Extra Years of Life." Presentation delivered at TED Global Conference, June 2012. http://www.ted.com/talks/

jane_mcgonigal_the_game_that_can_give_you_10_extra_years_
of_life.html.

MacRitchie, V., and S. Leibowitz. "Secondary Traumatic Stress, Level
of Exposure, Empathy and Social Support in Trauma Workers."
South African Journal of Psychology 40 (2010): 149–58.

Norris, F. H., and K. Kaniasty. "Received and Perceived Social Support in Times of Stress: A Test of the Social Support Deterioration
Deterrence Model." *Journal of Personality and Social Psychology*
71 (1996): 498–511.

NPR/TED staff. "Can Video Games Solve Real Issues?"
NPR/TED Radio Hour, May 21, 2012. http://www.npr
.org/2012/05/25/153235606/can-video-games-solve-real-issues.

Oxfam International. "A Year of Indecision Leaves Haiti's Recovery at a Standstill." Press release, 2011. http://
www.oxfam.org/en/pressroom/pressrelease/2011-01-06/
year-indecision-leaves-haiti-recovery-standstill.

Penninx, B. W. J. H., T. van Thilburg, D. M. W. Kriegsman, D. J. D.
Deeg, A. J. P. Boeke, and J. T. M. van Eikj. "Effects of Social Sup-
port and Personal Coping Resources on Mortality in Older Age:
The Longitudinal Aging Study Amsterdam." *American Journal of
Epidemiology* 146 (1997): 510–19.

Prati, G., and L. Pietrantoni. "Optimism, Social Support, and Coping
Strategies as Factors Contributing to Posttraumatic Growth: A
Meta-Analysis." *Journal of Loss and Trauma* 14 (2008): 364–88.

Weihs, K. L., T. M. Enright, and S. J. Simmens. "Close Relationships
and Emotional Processing Predict Decreased Mortality in Women
with Breast Cancer: Preliminary Evidence." *Psychosomatic Medicine* 70 (2008): 117–24.

Whitelocks, S. "Work-Related Stress Soared in the Recession as
Number of People Going off Sick Rose by a Quarter." *Daily Mail*,
February 22, 2012. http://www.dailymail.co.uk/health/article-
2104939/Work-related-stress-soared-recession-number-people
-going-sick-rose-quarter.html.

U.S. Geological Survey. "Haiti Dominates Earthquake Fatalities in 2010," 2011. http://www.usgs.gov/newsroom/article.asp?ID=2679.

CHAPTER 6

Becker, E. *Escape from Evil.* New York: Free Press, 1975.

Byock, I. Foreword in D. B. Feldman and S. A. Lasher, *The End-of-Life Handbook: A Compassionate Guide to Connecting with and Caring for a Dying Loved One.* Oakland, CA: New Harbinger, 2008, pp. v–viii.

Cozzolino, P. J. "Death Contemplation, Growth, and Defense: Converging Evidence of Dual-Existential Systems?" *Psychological Inquiry* 17 (2006): 278–87.

Cozzolino, P. J., A. D. Staples, L. S. Meyers, and J. Samboceti. "Greed, Death, and Values: From Terror Management to Transcendence Management Theory." *Personality and Social Psychology Bulletin* 30 (2004): 287–92.

Fernandez, S., E. Castano, and I. Singh. "Managing Death in the Burning Grounds of Varanasi, India: A Terror Management Investigation." *Journal of Cross-Cultural Psychology* 41 (2010): 182–94.

Gongloff, M. "Tracking Consumer Dollars, Sense." *CNN Money,* September 30, 2002. http://money.cnn.com/2002/09/27/news/economy/consumer/.

Hayes, J., J. Schimel, J. Arndt, and E. H. Faucher. "A Theoretical and Empirical Review of the Death-Thought Accessibility Concept in Terror Management Research." *Psychological Bulletin* 136 (2010): 699–739.

Heine, S. J., M. Harihara, and U. Niiya. "Terror Management in Japan." *Asian Journal of Social Psychology* 5 (2002): 187–96.

Jonas, E., I. Fritsche, and J. Greenberg. "Currencies as Cultural Symbols: An Existential Psychological Perspective on Reactions of Germans toward the Euro." *Journal of Economic Psychology* 26 (2005): 129–46.

Kart, J. "Abandoned House Becomes 'Before I Die' Wall of Dreams." Treehugger.com, May 9, 2011. http://www.treehugger.com/culture/abandoned-house-becomes-before-i-die-wall-of-dreams-photos.html.

Kasser, T., and K. M. Sheldon. "Of Wealth and Death: Materialism, Mortality Salience, and Consumption Behavior." *Psychological Science* 11 (2000): 348–51.

Lickerman, A. "Why We Laugh." *Psychology Today*, January 23, 2011. http://www.psychologytoday.com/blog/happiness-in-world/201101/why-we-laugh.

Matt, G. E., and C. Vázquez. "Anxiety, Depressed Mood, Self-Esteem, and Traumatic Stress Symptoms among Distant Witnesses of the 9/11 Terrorist Attacks: Transitory Responses and Psychological Resilience." *The Spanish Journal of Psychology* 11 (2008): 503–15.

Payne, E. "Group Apologizes to Gay Community, Shuts Down 'Cure' Ministry." CNN, July 8, 2013. http://www.cnn.com/2013/06/20/us/exodus-international-shutdown.

Pyszczynski, T., J. Greenberg, and S. Solomon. "Terror Management Theory of Self-Esteem." In C. R. Snyder and D. R. Forsyth, eds. *Handbook of Social and Clinical Psychology*. Elmsford, NY: Pergamon, 1991, pp. 21–40.

———. "Why Do We Need What We Need? A Terror Management Perspective on the Roots of Human Social Motivation." *Psychological Inquiry* 8 (1997): 1–20.

Routledge, C., and J. Juhu. "When Death Thoughts Lead to Death Fears: Mortality Salience Increases Death Anxiety for Individuals Who Lack Meaning in Life." *Cognition and Emotion* 24, no. 5 (2010).

Sani, F., M. Herrera, and M. Bowe. "Perceived Collective Continuity and Ingroup Identification as Defense against Death Awareness." *Journal of Experimental Social Psychology* 45 (2009): 242–45.

Solomon, S., J. Greenberg, and T. Pyszczynski. "Lethal Consumption: Death-Denying Materialism." In T. Kasser and Allen D. Kanner, eds. *Psychology and Consumer Culture: The Struggle for a Good*

Life in a Materialistic World. Washington, DC: American Psychological Association, 2004, pp. 127–46.

————. "A Terror Management Theory of Social Behavior: The Psychological Functions of Self-Esteem and Cultural Worldviews." *Advances in Experimental Social Psychology* 24 (1991): 93–159.

U.S. Department of Health and Human Services. "Advance Directives and Advance Care Planning: Report to Congress," 2008. http://aspe.hhs.gov/daltcp/reports/2008/ADCongRpt.pdf.

Vaes, J., N. A. Heflick, and J. L. Goldenberg. "'We Are People': Ingroup Humanization as an Existential Defense." *Journal of Personality and Social Psychology* 98 (2010): 750–60.

Weise, D. R., T. Arciszewski, J. Verlhiac, T. Pyszczynski, and J. Greenberg. "Terror Management and Attitudes toward Immigrants: Differential Effects of Mortality Salience for Low and High Right-Wing Authoritarians." *European Psychologist* 17 (2011): 63–72.

Winfrey, O. (host). "Rwandan Refugees Reunite with Their Family" [television broadcast]. September 4, 2009. http://www.oprah.com/spirit/Rwandan-Refugees-Reunite-with-Their-Family-Video.

CHAPTER 7

Bagwell, O. (executive producer), and S. Bellows, S. (senior producer). *Africans in America* [television broadcast]. WGBH-PBS, 1998.

Ben-Ezra, M., Y. Palgi, D. Sternberg, D. Berkley, H. Eldar, Y. Glidai, L. Moshe, and A. Shrira. "Losing My Religion: A Preliminary Study of Changes in Belief Pattern after Sexual Assault." *Traumatology* 16 (2010): 7–13.

Brown, L. S. *Cultural Competence in Trauma Therapy: Beyond the Flashback*. Washington, DC: American Psychological Association, 2008.

Bussee, M. Statement of Apology, 2007. http://www.beyondexgay.com/article/busseeapology.

Butler, S. M., and D. A. Snowdon. "Trends in Mortality in Older Women: Findings from the Nun Study." *Journal of Gerontology: Social Sciences* 51B (1996): S20I-S208.

Cameron, J. *A Time of Terror: A Survivor's Story.* Baltimore, MD: Black Classic Press, 1993.

Danner, D. D., D. A. Snowdon, and W. V. Friesen. "Positive Emotions in Early Life and Longevity: Findings from the Nun Study." *Journal of Personality and Social Psychology* 5 (2001): 804–13.

Fitchett, G., P. E. Murphy, J. Kim, J. L. Gibbons, J. R. Cameron, and J. A. Davis. "Religious Struggle: Prevalence, Correlates and Mental Health Risks in Diabetic, Congestive Heart Failure, and Oncology Patients." *International Journal of Psychiatry in Medicine* 34 (2004): 179–96.

Freud, S. *The Future of an Illusion.* New York: Norton, 1975.

Harris, J. I., C. R. Erbes, B. E. Engdahl, R. H. Olson, A. M. Winskowski, and J. McMahill. "Christian Religious Functioning and Trauma Outcomes." *Journal of Clinical Psychology* 64 (2008): 17–29.

Ironson, G., R. Stuetzle, D. Ironson, E. Balbin, H. Kremer, A. George, N. Schneiderman, and M. A. Fletcher. "View of God as Benevolent and Forgiving or Punishing and Judgmental Predicts HIV Disease Progression." *Journal of Behavioral Medicine* 34 (2011): 414–25.

Just the Facts Coalition. *Just the Facts about Sexual Orientation and Youth: A Primer for Principals, Educators, and School Personnel.* Washington, DC: American Psychological Association, 2008. http://www.apa.org/pi/lgbc/publications/justthefacts.html.

Lamb, Y. S. "Survived Lynching, Founded Museum" [obituary of James Cameron]. *The Washington Post,* June 13, 2006.

Levine, L. W. *Black Culture and Black Consciousness: Afro-American Folk Thought from Slavery to Freedom.* New York: Oxford University Press, 2007.

Levy, B. C., M. D. Slade, and P. Ranasinghe. "Causal Thinking after a Tsunami Wave: Karma Beliefs, Pessimistic Explanatory Style and Health among Sri Lankan Survivors." *Journal of Religion and Health* 48 (2009): 38–45.

Ling, L. (host). *Our America with Lisa Ling* [television broadcast]. Oprah Winfrey Network, June 20, 2013.

Marsh, C. *The Beloved Community: How Faith Shapes Social Justice, from the Civil Rights Movement to Today.* New York: Basic Books, 2004.

O'Grady, K. A., D. G. Rollison, T. S. Hanna, H. Schreiber-Pan, and M. A. Ruiz. "Earthquake in Haiti: Relationship with the Sacred in Times of Trauma." *Journal of Psychology and Theology* 40 (2012): 289–301.

Pargament, K. I., B. W. Smith, H. G. Koenig, and L. Perez. "Patterns of Positive and Negative Religious Coping with Major Life Stressors." *Journal for the Scientific Study of Religion* 37 (1998): 710–24.

Pargament, K. I., B. J. Zinnbauer, A. B. Scott, E. M. Butter, J. Zerowin, and P. Stanik. "Red Flags and Religious Coping: Identifying Some Religious Warning Signs among People in Crisis." *Journal of Clinical Psychology* 54 (1998): 77–89.

Park, C. L., J. H. Wortmann, and D. Edmondson. "Religious Struggle as a Predictor of Subsequent Mental and Physical Well-Being in Advanced Heart Failure Patients." *Journal of Behavioral Medicine* 34 (2011): 426–36.

Pirutinsky, S., D. H. Rosmarin, K. I. Pargament, and E. Midlarsky. "Does Negative Religious Coping Accompany, Precede, or Follow Depression among Orthodox Jews?" *Journal of Affective Disorders* 132 (2011): 401–5.

"Religion: Long-Live Nuns," *Time*, November 16, 1959. http://content.time.com/time/magazine/article/0,9171,811456,00.html.

Serovich, J. M., S. M. Craft, P. Toviessi, R. Gangamma, T. McDowell, and E. L. Grafsky. "A Systematic Review of the Research Base on

Sexual Reorientation Therapies." *Journal of Marital and Family Therapy* 34 (2008): 227–38.

Snowdon, D. *Aging with Grace: What the Nun Study Teaches Us about Leading Longer, Healthier, and More Meaningful Lives.* New York: Bantam, 2001.

Stewart, J. Y. "James Cameron, 92; Lynching Survivor Founded Black Holocaust Museum." *Los Angeles Times*, June 14, 2006. http://articles.latimes.com/2006/jun/14/local/me-cameron14/2.

Swarthout, G. *Bless the Beasts and Children.* New York: Simon and Schuster, 2004.

CHAPTER 8

Enright, R., and R. Fitzgibbons. *Helping Clients Forgive: An Empirical Guide for Resolving Anger and Restoring Hope.* Washington, DC: American Psychological Association, 2000.

Kamenev, M. "Rating Countries for the Happiness Factor." *Bloomberg BusinessWeek*, October 11, 2006. http://www.businessweek.com/stories/2006-10-11/rating-countries-for-the-happiness-factorbusinessweek-business-news-stock-market-and-financial-advice.

Kessler, R. C., A. Sonnega, E. Bromet, M. Hughes, and C. B. Nelson. "Posttraumatic Stress Disorder in the National Comorbidity Survey." *Archives of General Psychiatry* 52 (1995): 1048–60.

Messias, E., A. Saini, P. Sinato, and S. Welch. "Bearing Grudges and Physical Health: Relationship to Smoking, Cardiovascular Health and Ulcers." *Social Psychiatry and Psychiatric Epidemiology* 45 (2010): 183–87.

Stein, D. J., W. T. Chiu, I. Hwang, R. C. Kessler, N. Sampson, J. Alonso, M. K. Nock. "Cross-National Analysis of the Associations between Traumatic Events and Suicidal Behavior: Findings from the WHO World Mental Health Surveys." *PLoS ONE* 5 (2010). doi:10.1371/journal.pone.0010574.

Strelan, P., and T. Covic. "A Review of Forgiveness Process Models and a Coping Framework to Guide Future Research." *Journal of Social and Clinical Psychology* 25 (2006): 1059–85.

Thompson, L. Y., C. R. Snyder, L. Hoffman, S. T. Michael, H. N. Rasmussen, L. S. Billings, and D. E. Roberts. "Dispositional Forgiveness of Self, Others, and Situations." *Journal of Personality* 73 (2005): 313–59.

Tjaden, P., and N. Thoennes. "Full Report of the Prevalence, Incidence, and Consequences of Violence against Women: Findings from the National Violence against Women Survey, U.S. Department of Justice, 2000. http://www.ncjrs.gov/pdffiles1/nij/183781. pdf.

Toussaint, L. L., D. R. Williams, M. A. Musick, and S. A. Everson-Rose. "Why Forgiveness May Protect against Depression: Hopelessness as an Explanatory Mechanism." *Personality and Mental Health* 2 (2008): 89–103.

Vrana, S., and D. Lauterbach. "Prevalence of Traumatic Events and Post-Traumatic Psychological Symptoms in a Nonclinical Sample of College Students." *Journal of Traumatic Stress* 7 (1994): 289–302.

Wiesel, E. *Night*. New York: Bantam, 1982.

Witvliet, C. V., T. E. Ludwig, and K. L. Vander Laan. "Granting Forgiveness or Harboring Grudges: Implications for Emotion, Physiology, and Health." *Psychological Science* 12 (2001): 117–23.

Worthington, E. L., Jr., C. V. O. Witvliet, P. Pietrini, and A. J. Miller. "Forgiveness, Health, and Well-Being: A Review of Evidence for Emotional Versus Decisional Forgiveness, Dispositional Forgivingness, and Reduced Unforgiveness." *Journal of Behavioral Medicine* 30 (2007): 291–302.

CHAPTER 9

Helliker, K. "The Terminal Cancer Patient Who Won a Marathon." *The Wall Street Journal*, March 22, 2013. http://online.wsj.com/article/SB10001424127887323419104578374870179274496.html.

Iyengar, S. S., and E. Kamenica. "Choice Proliferation, Simplicity Seeking, and Asset Allocation." *Journal of Public Economics* 94 (2010): 530–39.

Iyengar, S. S., R. E. Wells, and B. Schwartz. "Doing Better but Feeling Worse: Looking for the 'Best' Job Undermines Satisfaction." *Psychological Science* 17 (2006): 143–50.

Lawler, P. "Big Idea: The Hell of Pure Possibility." *Bigthink.com*, 2012. http://bigthink.com/rightly-understood/big-idea-the-hell-of-pure-possibility.

Nisbett, R. E., and T. D. Wilson. "The Halo Effect: Evidence for Unconscious Alteration of Judgments." *Journal of Personality and Social Psychology* 4 (1977): 250–56.

Salecl, R. *The Tyranny of Choice*. London: Profile Books, 2011.

Schwartz, B. *The Paradox of Choice: Why More Is Less*. New York: Ecco, 2003.

———. "Self-Determination: The Tyranny of Freedom." *American Psychologist* 55 (2000): 79–88.

Thorndike, E. L. "A Constant Error in Psychological Ratings." *Journal of Applied Psychology* 4 (1920): 25–29.

Tversky, A., and E. Shafir. "Choice under Conflict: The Dynamics of Deferred Decision." *Psychological Science* 3 (1992): 358–61.

Zaleon, A. "Brain Cancer Patient Wins Gusher Marathon." *Beaumont Enterprise*, March 11, 2013. http://www.beaumontenterprise.com/sports/article/Brain-cancer-patient-wins-Gusher-Marathon-4342280.php.

EPILOGUE

Kessler, R. C., A. Sonnega, E. Bromet, M. Hughes, and C. B. Nelson. "Posttraumatic Stress Disorder in the National Comorbidity Survey." *Archives of General Psychiatry* 52 (1995): 1048–60.

Mitchell, G., and S. M. Darraj. *Máiread Corrigan and Betty Williams: Partners for Peace in Northern Ireland.* New York: Chelsea House, 2006.

Vrana, S., and D. Lauterbach. "Prevalence of Traumatic Events and Post-Traumatic Psychological Symptoms in a Nonclinical Sample of College Students." *Journal of Traumatic Stress* 7 (1994): 289–302.

Index

About the Authors

DAVID B. FELDMAN, PHD, is considered to be among the top experts on hope in the field of psychology. An associate professor of counseling psychology at Santa Clara University, he holds a PhD in clinical psychology from the University of Kansas and completed a postdoctoral fellowship with the VA Palo Alto Health Care System. Dr. Feldman is the author of two previous books, has written for *Psychology Today* and the *Huffington Post*, and has published numerous research articles. He lives in the San Francisco Bay Area.

www.davidfeldmanphd.com

LEE DANIEL KRAVETZ has a master's degree in counseling psychology and is a graduate of the University of Missouri–Columbia School of Journalism. He has written for *Psychology Today*, the *Huffington Post*, and the *New York Times*, among other publications. He lives in the San Francisco Bay Area with his wife and children.

www.leedanielkravetz.com